CREATIVE OIL TECHNIQUES

COLLINS

CREATIVE OIL TECHNIQUES

Practical Step-by-Step Projects

HarperCollinsPublishers

Front cover: Ted Gould; back cover: Madge Bright
page 1: Moira Huntly
page 3: Caroline Penny

First published in the UK in 1999 by
HarperCollins Publishers, London

Based on *The Art of Drawing and Painting*
© Eaglemoss Publications Ltd 1996

**A catalogue record for this book is available from the
British Library.**

ISBN 0 00 413382 X

Printed in Hong Kong

10 9 8 7 6 5 4 3 2 1

Contents

PART 1

Basics of Oil Painting

Oil – the flexible medium

There's something about the way oil paints mix on the palette and how they handle on the canvas that is enormously appealing.

Oil has a quite unjustified reputation for being difficult, but in many ways it is the most forgiving of all the painting media. Because it dries very slowly, it gives you plenty of time to think about your approach – and you have the valuable opportunity to rework the paint if you change your mind.

Oil painting is also less technique-led than, say, watercolour. This means that right from the start a would-be artist can produce pleasing images with a richness and depth of colour unmatched by any other medium.

In oil paints, the pigment is held in an oil-binding medium. This is usually linseed oil. The paint has a buttery consistency and is sup-plied in metal tubes. You can use the paint directly from the tube but it is usually thinned with turpentine, or a mixture of turpentine and linseed oil.

The choice of whether or not to thin the paint depends on the effect you're after. You can build it up carefully in a succession of thin layers or apply it directly as thick dabs of creamy, textured colour. The resulting picture surface is either smooth and glossy or thickly encrusted with swirling paint which holds every detail of brush, rag or knife.

Various surfaces (known as supports) are suitable: these include hardboard, canvas boards, stretched canvas and paper.

▲ **There are many finely worked details in this oil painting – note in particular the velvety qualities of the curtain and cushion, the coarse weave of the wicker chair and rug and the smoother surfaces of wall and patio.**
'Lunch time' by Rosemary Davies, canvas, 42 x 46in

Rag painting: vegetables in a bowl

Whether you've used oil paints before or are starting out with them, this project – working with rags rather than brushes – is fun to do and encourages you to paint freely. It's a good discipline to use a limited palette to start with, and this helps to keep costs down as well.

Use a piece of good quality cartridge paper pinned to a board. If you haven't got an easel, prop the board against a chair. You want to be at a comfortable distance from your subject – about 5ft. Position yourself so that you can look easily from the still life group to the paper. Leave enough room behind you so that you can step back from your painting from time to time.

Our artist chose a bowl of vegetables for this demonstration. You can either do the same or pick any interesting group of objects that appeals to you.

Keep to a still life to start with. This provides a subject for interpretation and makes a good picture – and there's no chance of it getting up and walking away.

◀ **The set-up** Note how the roughness of the cauliflower contrasts with the smoothness of the aubergine and the shiny glazed bowl.

The carrots and lemon bring warmth to the overall colour scheme, while the teacloth introduces a new texture and a dramatic design (it also reflects light up on to the bowl).

Cool, natural light from both sides illuminates the subject and creates interesting highlights.

▶ **1** Start with a simple underdrawing. Stand at a comfortable arm's length from the paper and use a piece of charcoal to sketch in basic forms and spaces. Remember your sketch is only an underdrawing, so don't get hung up on detail. Flick over it with a clean dry cloth to leave a 'ghost image' ready for painting.

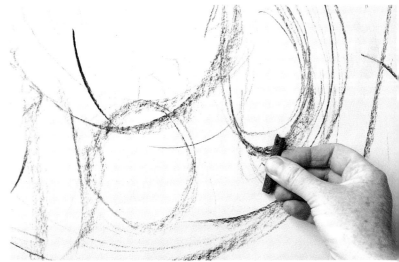

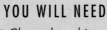

▲ **2** Scrunch up a piece of clean cotton rag in your hand. (Cotton rag is more absorbent than synthetic material. But make sure that it has no loose fibres which will stick to the painting.)

Dip the rag into the turps and moisten the cloth. As a rough guide, just dampen the area of the rag that you want to use so that the turps doesn't run down your arm.

Use the rag to thin down some red paint on the palette. Don't do the whole lot in one go – just nick a little from the main blob and thin that by working in the turps. Make the paint fairly turpsy – the paper tends to absorb the turps as you work.

▲ **3** Use the rag to rub in the red for the carrots. Do the same with yellow for the lemons and Hooker's green for the cauliflower leaves. Use a new part of the rag for each area so you keep the colours clean.

◄ **4** For the cauliflower – which is mainly white – leave the paper to show through. Mix a little raw sienna with white to make a pale brown. Use this and a touch of cobalt blue to suggest the darks on the cauliflower.

Leave the aubergine – the darkest object – until more of the mid tones have been established. The table top is important, so rub that in with Payne's gray.

YOU WILL NEED

- ☐ *Clean dry white cotton rags*
- ☐ *A 20 x 30in sheet of white cartridge paper*
- ☐ *Wooden board*
- ☐ *Charcoal*
- ☐ *Spirits of turpentine (turps substitute is good enough for this exercise)*
- ☐ *Dipper (container) for the turps*
- ☐ *Small tubes of students' grade paints: white, cadmium red, cadmium yellow, cobalt blue, Payne's gray, Hooker's green, raw sienna*
- ☐ *Palettes and toilet roll cylinder*

Tip

Clean turps

Pour only a little turps at a time. If you are using a shallow dish, for example, pour just enough to cover the bottom of the dish. Replace it with fresh turps before it starts to get muddy. This helps to keep colours clean and prevents unnecessary waste of turps.

▶ **5** Screw up your eyes and look at the light and dark areas in your subject. Try to match these in your painting.

Lighten some Payne's gray with white and use it to paint in the mid tones on the inside of the bowl. Overpaint this with cobalt blue lightened with white. Paint in the grey shadow under the bowl to describe the rim.

Use cobalt blue for the aubergine and fill in the dark area with Payne's gray. Use the same grey for the shadow between the carrots.

Notice how the red from the carrot has been used to shade the lemon, while the lemon lends the vaguest hint of yellow to the carrot.

◀ **6** Use your finger to build up a rich crunchy texture with white. (The light area on the cauliflower calls for a thicker ladling of paint – a turpsy rag tends to make it all a bit too thin.)

Don't worry about the white mixing with colours already on the paper – you don't want an unmodified white here anyway, and the mixing adds to the overall effect and texture.

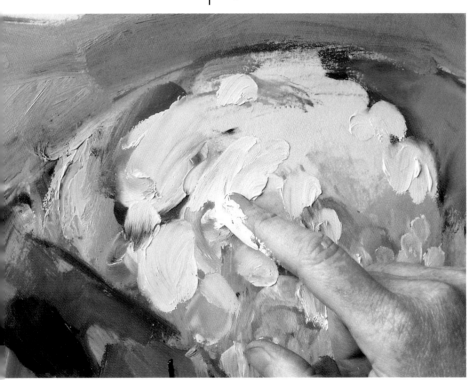

▶ **7** Look closely at the colours in your subject. Mix some of the same yellow as the lemon into the green of the cauliflower leaves. Tone down the red in the carrots by mixing in a touch of white. Leave a darker red to represent shade. A subtle smudge of warm pink brown on the aubergine turns this dark shape into a shiny, solid object. Make up this colour by mixing a little raw sienna, cadmium red and white.

Notice how the cloth forms a deep bank of shade behind the bowl.

▶ **8** Use the edge at the end of a flattened cardboard toilet roll cylinder (or any other thin piece of cardboard) to describe the florets on the cauliflower.

Pick up the red of the carrots and yellow from the lemon, but notice too how the artist has actually left an impression in the surface – removing paint at the same time as adding it.

Now stand back and have a look. The artist decided that the inside of the bowl was too dark, and used a Payne's gray with some white to lighten it.

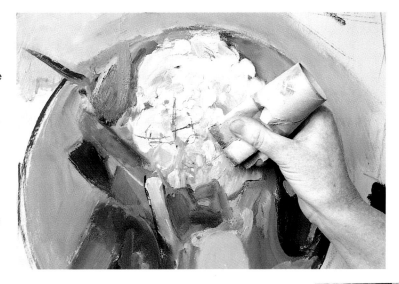

Tip

▼ **9** A mere touch of outline serves to strengthen the composition. Use Payne's gray and cobalt blue to define parts of the oval rim and to suggest the stalkiness of the cauliflower leaves.

See how the colours are really working within the bowl now. Yellow from the cauliflower leaves is reflected at the back and red from the carrots at the front.

Mixing on palette
When mixing colours on a palette (above) it's important to keep them clean. Don't mix patches of colour too close together – keep them separate. Once you have mixed a new colour, keep a little of it on one side without adding any others to it. You may want to use it again later and it's next to impossible to mix exactly the same colour again.

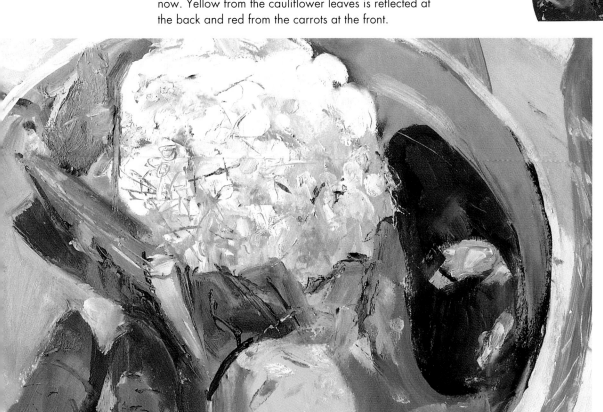

►10 Use a pale cobalt blue for the stripes on the tea cloth. Don't attempt to describe intricate designs. Here the artist puts in flecks of white to suggest detail on the stripes.

A few carefully observed highlights help to make the surface of the lemon really sing and lend form to the aubergine and the inside of the bowl.

▼11 Your painting is finished when you are happy with the result. Here the artist removes one stripe to simplify the picture. But the area of cloth wasn't just left a blank white. Instead the artist used pale greys and greens to break up the cloth, making the whole surface of the painting more exciting to look at.

SOLVE IT

Chop and change

The beauty with oil is that you can make changes at any stage. After leaving the painting for a couple of hours, the artist decided to simplify the foreground by removing a stripe on the tea cloth with a clean piece of rag and some white to cover the blue.

Checking up on oil paints

To get the best out of your paints, it helps to know what their special qualities are and how to exploit both their advantages AND their disadvantages.

Easy to work with and readily available, oil paints are extremely versatile, allowing you to create a wide range of superb effects. You can use them straight from the tube to make exciting, thickly textured impasto works in a single day, or dilute them with a medium to create layers of scumbles and glazes (which take rather longer). Opaque and transparent oil paints are available to increase your options further.

What are oil paints?

Generally, identical pigments – made from earth materials, minerals, plant extracts and synthetic chemicals – are used in oils, acrylic and watercolours. The difference comes in the binder (or medium) that holds the pigment together and sticks it to the support. Linseed oil, the binding agent used in most of today's oil paints, gives an unparalleled richness of colour.

► Colour selection is an individual matter, but you need both warm and cool colours for versatility. This all-purpose basic palette has a warm and a cool blue, and the same for red and yellow. An earthy green (oxide of chromium) and a sharp green (viridian) produce a wide range of colours for landscapes. White, black and two warm earth colours are also invaluable.

▼ Many artists arrange the paints on their palette from warm to cool colours (or vice versa). Always put your paints in the same order so you automatically know where to dip your brush.

The trays (dippers) can contain turps, linseed oil or a medium. Use a separate, larger container of white spirit for cleaning brushes.

viridian

oxide of chromium

French ultramarine

cerulean blue

alizarin crimson

cadmium red

lemon yellow

cadmium yellow

burnt umber

raw sienna

lamp black

titanium white

An all-round landscape palette

If you know you want to paint particular subjects, then choose your palette accordingly. For example, an all-round landscape palette has earthy colours – yellow ochre and Vandyke brown – along with natural-looking greens (viridian and sap green) for foliage. Use warm and cool blues, white and cadmium yellow on their own or mix them to create other colours. Here, from left to right, are: viridian, sap green, cobalt blue, cerulean blue, cadmium yellow, yellow ochre, Vandyke brown, ivory black.

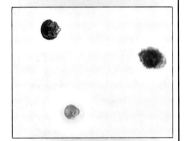
Some art scholars reckon that artists in Germany in the 12th century were already mixing their pigments with linseed oil. But it was the 15th century Flemish master, Jan van Eyck, who really made oil paints popular.

A special character

Oil paints dry very slowly (unlike watercolour, acrylic and gouache which are water-based). Depending on the thickness of the paint, oils stay wet and workable for quite a long time, allowing you to try again – or use a different technique – if you aren't getting just the effect you want.

This means that, unlike watercolour work, you don't have the pressure of getting the painting right first time. All you need do is simply wipe the paint off or add another layer over the first one. You can even scrape off thick paint with a knife and put it back on the palette – something unique to oils. And if the paint is thin, you can wipe it off with a rag soaked in white spirit. Finally, you can blend colours together and work wet-in-wet for a long while.

▼ The colours in the foreground (the figures) are sharp and pure. The artist has used oils in a completely traditional way, building up subtle skin tones with many glazes. To knock them back, background colours are mixed with white and complementaries.

The modern equivalent palette colours shown here, reading from top to bottom, are: lamp black, Prussian blue, purple madder, alizarin crimson, Venetian red, chrome yellow deep, burnt umber, raw sienna and sap green.

'Family of Darius before Alexander the Great' by Paolo Veronese, oil on canvas, 93 x 187in

It must be said, though, that working quickly with oils can be frustrating. For instance, the colours could blend together if you add a second glaze too quickly over a wet first layer. There's nothing for it but to wait until it dries – unless you wish to exploit or harness the effect in some way.

Using oils

Good quality paints have a class or star system to rate their permanence. Class AA (or three star) colours are permanent and very stable, while class C are fugitive (they fade quickly). Some colours contain hazardous materials, so don't get the paint on your fingers.

You thin oil paint with turpentine and/or linseed oil – don't use white spirit because it isn't entirely compatible with oil paints. You can wash your brushes in white spirit, then use soap and warm water or washing-up liquid, and rinse under the tap. Use a cotton rag soaked in white spirit to wipe paint off your hands. Some people are allergic to turps and white spirit. Other products are available, but they're expensive.

► Viridian is a cool, sharp green. Here it is used unmixed and also diluted with white to set up a bold contrast with the warm red. In much of the painting the colour is scumbled so the texture of the canvas shows through, but there are also many areas of thick impasto.

The equivalent modern palette colours, shown from top to bottom, are: cobalt blue, cerulean blue, cadmium red, yellow ochre, chrome orange, cadmium yellow, viridian and permanent green.

'Young girls in the Garden at Montmartre' by Pierre-Auguste Renoir, oil on canvas, 21 ¼ x 25 ½ in

◄ Van Gogh's particular genius was to see – and use – colours in a heightened way. He used many straight from the tube, often enhancing the natural colour of his subject and thereby intensifying its impact. The blues here are used in pure form or mixed with white. Predominant in the sunflowers is Naples yellow, its chalky opacity contrasting well with the transparent viridian.

Modern palette equivalents, from top to bottom, are: cobalt blue, cerulean blue, Prussian blue, viridian, yellow ochre, Naples yellow, alizarin crimson.

'Sunflowers' by Vincent van Gogh, 1887, oil on canvas, 17 x 24in (Metropolitan Museum of Art)

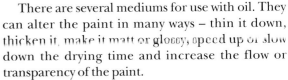

◀ The mostly dark background does much to bring this colourful dancer forward in the picture. The reds sparkle against the black of the skirt and the green-grey of the floor, and a thin scumble of opaque white suggests the crunchy texture of the lace veil. Modern palette equivalents, from top to bottom, are: lamp black, Payne's gray, cobalt blue, sap green, alizarin crimson, cadmium red, permanent rose, yellow ochre and raw sienna.
'Lola de Valence' by Edouard Manet, oil on canvas, 123 x 92cm (Musée d'Orsay, Paris)

Check in your local art shop for suitable alternatives. Whether you're allergic to turps or white spirit or not, work in a well ventilated room.

There are several mediums for use with oil. They can alter the paint in many ways – thin it down, thicken it, make it matt or glossy, speed up or slow down the drying time and increase the flow or transparency of the paint.

It takes a while to get used to all these different mediums, and not even professional artists know exactly what they all do. Many artists use 'fast-drying'

▼ Hot, intense colours glow in this painting – they aren't dirtied or knocked back by mixing with earth colours or complementaries, and you can see raw canvas between dabs of pure colour. Optical colour mixing occurs in the viewer's eyes, making for a shimmering surface.

Modern palette equivalents, top to bottom: ultramarine, cobalt blue, rose madder, deep yellow, golden ochre, transparent golden ochre, Prussian green and olive green.
'Houses of Parliament' by André Derain, 1905-6, oil on canvas, 31 ⅛ x 38 ⅝in, (© ADAGP, Paris and DACS, London 1994)

▲ The artist here has chosen his reds with great care. The warm reds — oranges and dusky pinks — are concentrated in the centre, around the light source (the lamp), but the cooler reds start to appear as you move away towards the edges (particularly in the bottom right corner).

Modern palette equivalents, from top to bottom, are: viridian, ultramarine, cadmium yellow, cadmium red, rose madder and ivory black.

'Intérieur with Mme Vuillard' by Edouard Vuillard , 1893-95

► Cool blue-grey neutrals contrast with the bright yellows of the daffodils and the warm, earthy, sienna-based colour on the windowsill.

Great delicacy of touch is evident here, both in the very thin layers of paint used in the background and on the windowsill and in the more generous application of paint on the daffodil heads and sprays of honesty.

Palette colours, from top to bottom, are: aureolin yellow, lemon yellow, yellow ochre, cerulean blue, ultramarine, cadmium red, alizarin crimson and burnt sienna.

'Spring daffodils, Mousehole' by Ken Howard , oil on canvas, 24 x 20in alkyd mediums such as Wingel or Liquin from Winsor & Newton to speed up the paint's drying time and extend its flow. Manufacturers don't all use the same names, so ask for more information in an art shop.

Supports, brushes, palettes

Canvas is the most popular support for oils, but hardboard, millboard and cardboard are all suitable surfaces. You should treat all supports before you begin painting (unless you buy them ready prepared). If oil paint is applied to an absorbent support, the surface soaks up the oil from the paint and can rot it.

Brushes come in a wide range of shapes, sizes and materials. In general, brushes for oils are made of synthetic fibres and bristle hair – both are hard wearing. Their long handles mean you can work at a distance from the easel and see what you're doing.

Your palette should be smooth, flat and non-absorbent. A ceramic plate, a sheet of coated hardboard or plate glass, plastic, melamine or Formica is fine. You can also buy pads of non-absorbent, disposable paper palettes.

▼ A range of earthy colours in this landscape are offset by a number of cool greys – in the trees on the horizon, the distant hills, the rooftops and the car in the foreground. The road is a soft grey, made from mixing complementary colours; patches of the toned ground show through to warm the whole scene. The season is early spring – cool, but with the promise of returning warmth.
'Stoneswood, Delph, Early Spring' by John McCombs, oil on canvas, 14 ⅛ x 13 ¼in

Palette colours, top to bottom: chrome yellow, yellow ochre, chrome orange, flesh tint, alizarin crimson, burnt sienna, Vandyke brown, sap green, Prussian blue.

Essential oils

To create thick, custardy impastos, oil paints can be applied raw to the canvas. In general, however, you need to add an oil medium to the paint to increase its fluidity and improve the way it handles.

Mediums are fluids, gels or pastes – usually oils or oil-derived – added to oil paint to change its character. Essentially, they enable you to create a variety of depths and textures in your paintings. However, different mediums have different qualities, and it is important to choose the right medium if you want to obtain a particular effect. Some mediums can thin paint to make it less opaque (especially good for creating transparent glazes). Others give the paint more body so that it holds the mark of the brush or knife, or vary the rate at which the paint dries (useful if you want to work wet-in-wet). Most important of all, perhaps, many increase the flow of the paint so that you can achieve smooth, blended effects without visible brushmarks.

Here we provide a general survey of the most commonly used oil mediums, together with a number of lesser known synthetic additives.

▼► **Art shops stock a vast array of mediums for the oil painter. They can slow or speed drying times, add body or thin the paint, and they can even enhance the colour by preventing it from drying duller.**

Drying oils

Oils added to oil paint to change the way it behaves are called drying oils. The most popular is linseed oil, which is extracted from the seeds of the flax plant. There are several kinds available.

Cold-pressed linseed oil is the best quality, and is extracted from the first pressing of the flax seeds without the use of heat. The process produces a smaller quantity of oil but it is the purest and therefore the best to use as a painting medium. It's also the most expensive.

Refined linseed oil is a good alternative to cold pressed oil. It thins oil colour, increases gloss and transparency, and helps to slow down the drying time of the paint.

Sun-bleached linseed oil is a pale oil which dries slightly faster than refined linseed oil. It's particularly useful with pale colours and white, which might be muddied by darker oils.

Sun-thickened linseed oil is a slightly thicker version of sun-bleached oil and is sometimes known as 'fat oil'. It has a honey-like consistency and is used to improve the flow and handling of oil colours. It has good transparency and is fast drying, producing an enamel-like finish. It was favoured by Rubens.

Stand linseed oil is sometimes called 'boiled linseed oil'. It is a pale, thick oil produced by heating in an air-free container, and it dries to a tough, elastic film. It reduces brushmarks and does not yellow as much as other linseed oils.

Poppy oil is a common oil medium. It is a pale, slow-drying oil obtained from the pressed seeds of the white opium poppy. Because it does not yellow as much as linseed oil, it's used as a

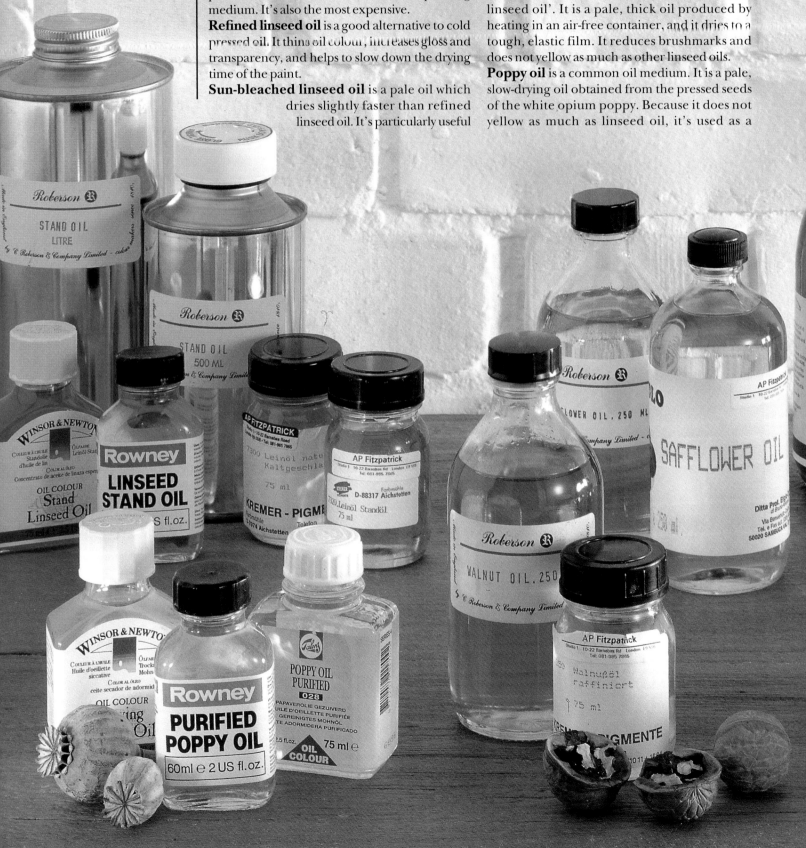

medium in situations when it is important not to darken the paint. It has a 'buttery' consistency which makes it especially suitable for *alla prima* painting because it holds the mark of the brush. Its slow drying time means it isn't suitable for paintings built up in layers, but it's ideal if you want to work wet-in-wet over a long period. Some of the Impressionists used poppy oil. **Walnut oil** was used in the early Renaissance period. The art historian Vasari (1511-71) recommended it because it yellowed less than linseed oil. It's a pale, thin oil, more fluid than linseed oil and a better drier than poppy oil.

Linseed and turpentine medium

This is perhaps the simplest and most common of all the painting mediums, and you mix it yourself. The proportions of each used depend on the preferences of the artist. If you are intending to build up several paint layers you should remember the 'fat over lean' rule and increase the proportion of oil in the topmost layers.

Alkyd mediums

These are synthetic resins prepared from a number of different ingredients. They are combined with drying oils to create a range of mediums which are generally characterized by their fast drying times, but like the oil mediums, each has different qualities.

Liquin (made by Winsor & Newton) is a quick-drying gel medium that improves the flow and transparency of paint. Used for thinning paint and thin glazes, it's easy to control – it doesn't trickle – and it gives the surface a glossy finish.

Wingel (made by Winsor & Newton) is a general purpose quick-drying medium with a jelly-like consistency. It changes its nature and behaviour when manipulated with the knife, becoming a free-flowing liquid. In this form it is used to create smooth textures and transparent glazes.

Oleopasto (also by Winsor & Newton) is another jelly-like, quick-drying medium. Designed specifically for knife-painting, it acts as a paint extender, allowing you to build up thick paint layers without using large quantities of expensive paint. It dries to a matt sheen.

Patent mediums

Manufacturers produce a wide range of mediums mixed from a variety of substances.

Artists' painting medium is a general purpose medium made from stand linseed oil. It thins oils, has good resistance to yellowing and cracking, and can be used to oil out dull patches.

Oil vehicle No 1A by Winsor & Newton is a thinning medium; it improves the flow and drying of oils.

Oil vehicle No 2A by Winsor & Newton is a thinning medium for pale oil and alkyd colours. It improves flow and dries more slowly than 1A.

Opal medium, made from beeswax and stand linseed oil, imparts a matt effect to oils and alkyds. It is slow drying.

Artists' matt medium gives a matt effect to oils and alkyds and forms a more durable film than wax-based mediums.

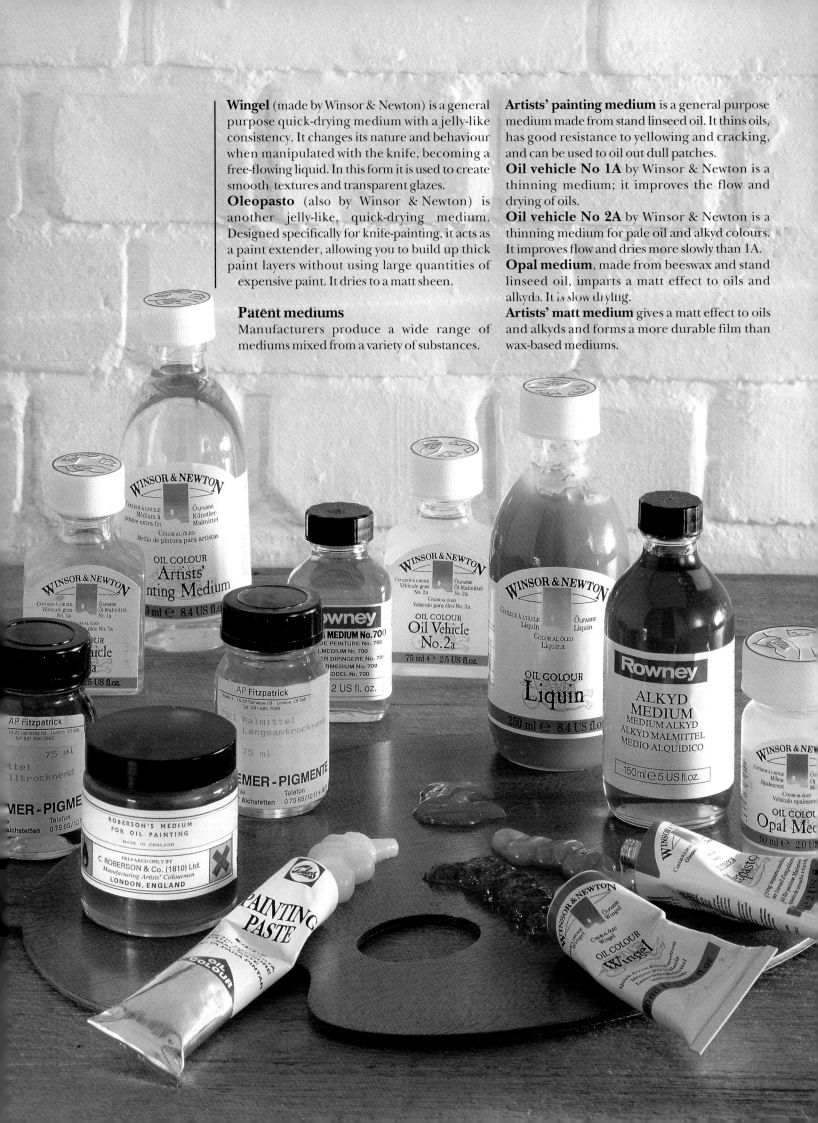

Thinners and cleaners

The right thinners and cleaners can affect the look and durability of your paintings – they don't just keep your brushes in good order – so it really pays to choose the right one for the right job.

If you look around any large art or craft shop, you'll find a bewildering display of different solvents, diluents and mediums, many of which appear to do much the same basic job but with slight variations.

The terms 'solvent', 'diluent' and 'medium' are hard to define because they often overlap in their uses, but for our purposes we'll define a solvent as a cleaner which dissolves oil paint; a diluent as a thinner; and a medium as any of the remaining substances which are used to change the texture, drying time or flow of paint. Do bear in mind that some substances are, of course, both solvent and diluent – turps is one such.

Diluents

These are used to thin paint so that it flows easily and spreads thinly. Starting off with thinned paint is part of the process of traditional oil painting. You simply dip your brush into the diluent and mix it in with the paint on your palette to the required consistency.

Many painters start with thin paint and gradually build up to thicker and richer paint by adding oil. Paint thinned with turpentine is said to be lean. Paint rich in oil (and therefore with less turpentine in it) is said to be fat. Once you've started with fat paint, you shouldn't use thin paint over it, no matter how thinly you've brushed out

▼ The range of thinners and cleaners is not as complicated as you might think. Turps is the best thinner and white spirit is the most economical cleaner. The only time you might want to use anything else is if you are allergic to one or the other, or if you dislike the smell.

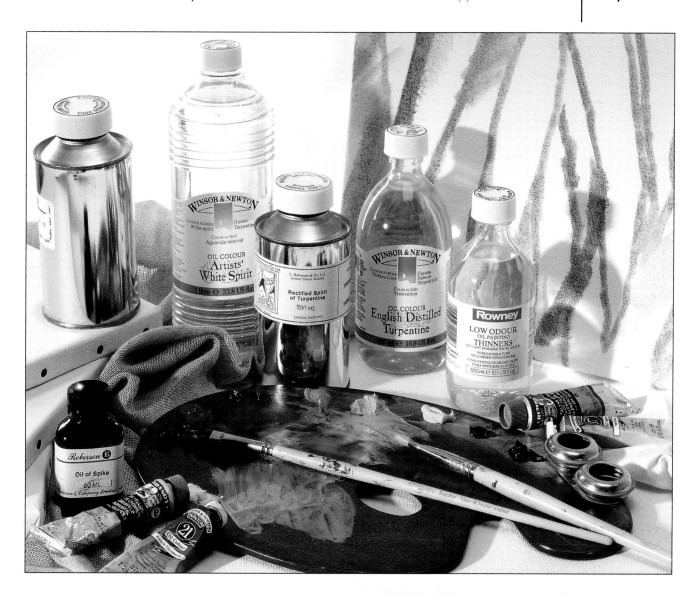

Tip

Save it!
Don't automatically throw away your muddy turpentine at the end of a painting

1

2

session. If you've got a lot in the jar (1), leave it to stand overnight so the paint sinks, then pour off the clean turps left at the top (2).

the thick paint. This is because paint mixed with turpentine dries much more quickly than paint mixed with oil and turps. So if you put lean paint over fat, the top layer will dry before the bottom layer, causing the painting to crack.

Thinned paint is also more practical to start off with. It dries more quickly and is more workable than thick paint, and it flows more easily, enabling you to make a brush drawing or underpainting without using too much paint. You can also move shapes around and adjust the major elements in the composition without creating tell-tale ridges where the edges of a shape used to be.

Turpentine is the best diluent or thinner for oil paint. It's a clear, colourless liquid which is compatible with oil paint and all proprietary oil paint mediums, such as linseed oil and Liquin. It is known by several names: spirit of turpentine, oil of turpentine or genuine turpentine. The best quality is called rectified or double distilled turpentine, but pure gum spirits of turpentine should serve just as well. Turpentine evaporates quite quickly, leaving a negligible residue, and it should be stored in a completely air-tight – preferably child-proof – container.

Turpentine is a natural product, made by distilling the resinous sap of pine trees or similar coniferous trees – the best grades can still contain traces of the resin. It has a distinctive – some would say highly agreeable – odour which often lingers in the artist's studio. Because its smell is quite strong, some people find it gives them headaches or causes

dizziness. If you wish to paint indoors and turpentine affects you in this way, keep a window open, take regular walks outside or use a turpentine substitute (see below).

White spirit, developed as a cheaper substitute for turpentine, is a clear, colourless liquid distilled from petroleum oil. It has a mild smell and it evaporates at speed, leaving no residue, and it doesn't deteriorate with age.

It is sometimes used as a diluent, but, although you can use it for this purpose, most artists would advise against it because white spirit is not as compatible with oil paints as turpentine. Artists are always aware that their paintings should stand the test of time, and want to avoid the paint cracking in three, thirty or three hundred years time. You may think this is unimportant for your first daubs and experiments, but you should get into good habits right from the beginning. No one will know if you use white spirit instead of turpentine to thin your paint, but you may regret it at a later date. Don't risk your painting by saving a few pennies.

Turpentine substitutes are invaluable if you are allergic to turpentine or white spirit or if you simply dislike the smell of turpentine. Some of them, such as oil of spike lavender, were in use before turpentine came to favour.

Low-odour thinner (Rowney) and Sansodor (Winsor & Newton), are, as their names suggest, more or less odour-free. Low-odour thinner has the same sort of evaporation rate as turpentine, making it a good general alternative. Sansodor is slow drying, and

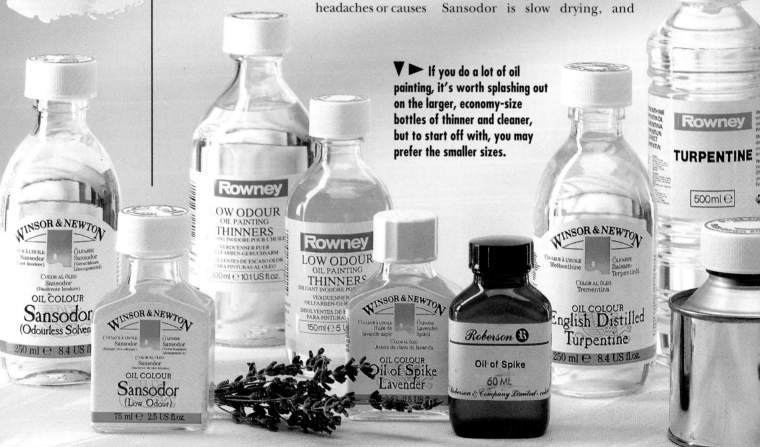

▼ ► If you do a lot of oil painting, it's worth splashing out on the larger, economy-size bottles of thinner and cleaner, but to start off with, you may prefer the smaller sizes.

therefore useful when you want more control. Both thinners are compatible with oil paints, but they are more expensive than turpentine.

Oil of spike lavender is made from the stems of lavender plants. It has a strong smell and is a powerful solvent. It is more resinous (oily) than turps and takes longer to evaporate, making it good for *alla prima* techniques since the paint remains in a workable state for longer.

You may also come across Venice turpentine, a medium in use for centuries but now not so common. This is not a paint thinner, but a thick resin tapped from larch trees. It has a characteristic odour of pine and is used mainly as a glaze medium, varnish or adhesive.

Solvents

It's important to clean your brushes, knives and palettes at once to ensure they last. Sable brushes, in particular, benefit from careful treatment, since they won't last long if paint is left on them, and they're too expensive to replace regularly.

Wipes and cleaners

▲ Wipes impregnated with solvent are a convenient option. Simply pull one out of the tub, tear it off, and then use it to wipe your brushes, palette and hands clean. Rinse your brushes in warm, soapy water.

▲ If you're using a gel or liquid cleaner, put a little in your palm and gently massage the brush in it. Then rinse your brush and hands in warm, soapy water. A barrier cream, such as Artguard protects your hands from being stained by paint. Wash it off with soapy water or a cleaner.

Turpentine is the best solvent and diluent for oil painting, but it works out quite expensive if you're doing a lot of painting, so it makes sense to use a cheaper alternative for such ordinary jobs as cleaning your brushes and palettes.

White spirit is one of the cheapest solvents around, and it's widely available. You can buy it from art shops and hardware shops (where it's sold for cleaning brushes and rollers used with oil-based household paints). If you're doing a lot of painting, a large plastic container is more economical than a small glass bottle.

There are several other products available for cleaning your brushes, palettes and hands which you might prefer if you have sensitive skin. Both turps and white spirit can cause skin rashes – or worse on very sensitive skins. There's a barrier cream which will prevent your hands from becoming stained by paint, and a cleaner in gel form which helps to remoisturise your hands. For easy cleaning, you can buy tissues, such as Winsor & Newton's Artwipes, which are impregnated with solvent.

▲ Single and double dippers (with or without lids) are handy, shallow metal containers which you can clip on to the side of your palette. With a double dipper, you can decant some turpentine into one container and a medium into the other.

Health and safety

White spirit and turpentine are volatile; that is to say, they evaporate readily into the atmosphere. The vapours shouldn't be breathed in for long periods in unventilated rooms. Keep the window open if you are working indoors, or take walks outside.

Both turps and white spirit are also flammable. You are advised not to eat, drink or smoke in a studio when turps or white spirit is being used – although these precautions are probably ignored by most artists.

Containers

It's a good idea to decant some turpentine into a small container so that you don't 'dirty' your main supply. Some people like to use a single or double dipper which can be conveniently clipped on to your palette. With a double dipper you can use one container for turps and the other for a medium. You'll also need a jar of white spirit for cleaning your brushes. If you don't have a dipper, pour turps into a screw-top glass jar – a container with a top will prevent white spirit and turpentine evaporating. Don't use a plastic cup or old margarine pot – after a while the white spirit or turps eats into the plastic and you'll find it has all leaked out!

▲ Many dippers don't have lids, so you can't save the contents between sessions. To avoid waste, just put a little turpentine in the dipper – you can always top it up if you need to. Clean out the dipper after use, otherwise your clean turpentine will be dirtied the moment you pour it in.

Bristle brushes for oil

Brushes – the artist's main tool for applying oil paint – are available in an enormous range of shapes, sizes and materials. Choosing the right one for the job is vital for good results.

◀ **Energetic brushstrokes give life and texture to this painting. Long horizontal strokes and short stabs of colour in the foreground foliage create a great feeling of vigour and growth.**

The smoother, less defined strokes in the background aim for impression rather than detail, pushing the hills and trees back, suggesting space and distance.
'Banks of the river Tame, Delph, late summer' by John McCombs, 1991, 11³⁄₈ x 16¹⁄₄in

▼ **This detail of the stream shows how the broad horizontal strokes used to depict water also convey a feeling of calm and serenity.**

Every type of brush is suited to one or more tasks and each leaves a different kind of mark. Since they vary greatly in cost as well as versatility, you must choose your basic kit carefully.

When you are selecting brushes, don't feel daunted by the large choice available. You don't need a huge variety – start with three or four that satisfy your initial needs. One artist may use a dozen or more, but another may be perfectly happy with just a few selected brushes. It all depends on the techniques and the effects you want to achieve. So experiment to get a feel for what suits you, and gradually add to your collection of brushes as the need arises.

Types of brushes

Oil painting brushes are made from either bristles or soft hairs (or synthetic substitutes for them). Each has a specific function. Bristle brushes are good for establishing the initial stages of composition and laying in large amounts of colour. Their stiff bristles make them ideal for impasto work. Soft hair brushes are useful for smoother lines and precise details, and are often used for smaller paintings. Restrict yourself to bristle brushes when you are starting out. They encourage you to work loosely, which is valuable in the early stages of composition.

Bristle brushes

Stiff and hard-wearing, each strand of a bristle brush has split ends that hold large quantities of paint. It's a useful brush for making bold, decisive strokes; bigger sizes are good for covering broad areas with thick colour. It's also ideal for larger paintings, but its point is too stiff for details.

Traditionally, bristle brushes are made of hog's hair, which is particularly suitable for oil painting since the strength and flexibility of the bristles are good for the thick, heavy texture of the paint. Look for ones that have plenty of spring and keep their shape when you make a

stroke on your hand with them. Avoid synthetic substitutes, which are usually made of nylon and rapidly lose their shape.

Bristle brushes are available in some interesting shapes, but the four most useful ones are flats, brights, rounds and filberts.

Flats are extremely versatile brushes and essential for any basic collection. They have flat ends and long bristles that hold a lot of fluid paint. This makes them ideal for applying broad, rectangular strokes and areas of thick, bold colour, as well as for short dabs of colour. You can use the side of the brush for thin lines and sharp details. Flats are especially suitable for working up to a clean edge and blending areas of colour. Bear in mind that, since the bristles are quite elastic, they won't pick up stiff paint.

The brushes in the picture have been chosen because they make a good, all-purpose range of strokes and marks

Flats – Nos.12, 5 & 2

Flat brushes are good for laying in large areas of colour. The side is good for narrow lines, while the flat of the brush can be used for blocks of colour. Flats are good for blending paint and moving it around the canvas.

Rounds – Nos. 8, 4 & 2

These are good general-purpose brushes. They can be used for laying in broad areas of colour and for scumbling, and the tip of small sizes can be used for fine line work and small dabs of colour.

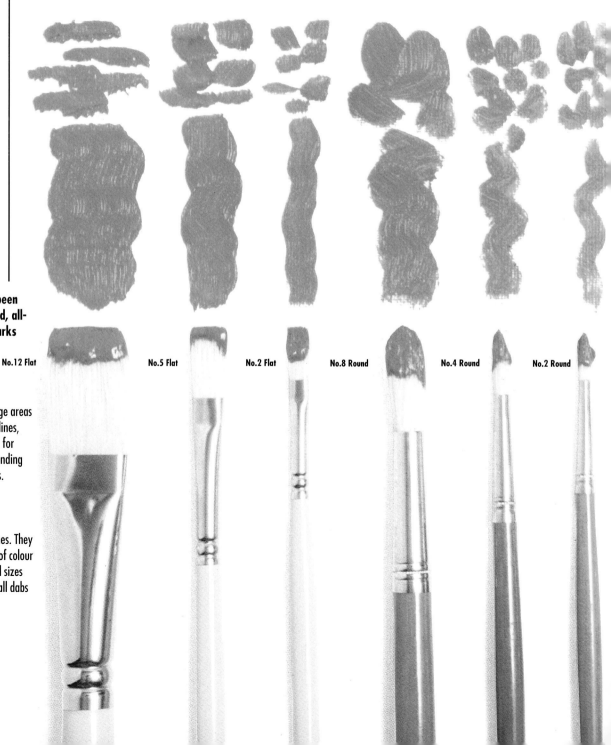

No.12 Flat   No.5 Flat   No.2 Flat   No.8 Round   No.4 Round   No.2 Round

Brights (sometimes called short flats) are the same shape as flats but with shorter, stiffer bristles that dig deeper into the paint and leave strongly textured, chunky marks. You'll find them useful if you want to apply stiff, thick paint to create impasto effects. Because of their shorter bristles brights are easier to control, making them better for moving in on details following a more generalized underpainting.

Rounds are exceptionally versatile brushes, indispensable in your basic kit. They have long, thin bristles that curve inwards at the ends. With heavily diluted paint, round brushes make soft, thin strokes that are ideal for establishing basic composition in the initial stage of a painting. Alternatively, by loading the brush with a lot of paint, you can make long, bold marks and lay in large areas of colour. Rounds are good for the technique of glazing, and also for delicate lines and outlines.

Filberts are similar to flats – they have a flat ferrule but curve inwards at the end. They are available in two versions. Filberts with long, springy bristles hold a lot of paint and make soft, tapered strokes. The other type, with short bristles, hold less paint and are easier to control – ideal for applying small dabs of colour. Tastes differ, but filberts are generally considered useful but not essential brushes.

Brush sizes

Each type of brush is made in a range of sizes, with each manufacturer offering their own range and numbering system. There are usually 12 sizes

▲ Decorators' brushes – ½in and 1in
Decorators' brushes are cheap, hard wearing and extremely useful. Because they have many bristles, you can load the brush heavily with paint to cover the entire canvas with a single wash. Or you can use them to block in large areas of colour for a bold underpainting.

Filberts – Nos. 12, 8 (short) & 2 (long)
Filberts produce a wide range of marks. The shape of the tip helps you avoid the blocky, rectangular marks sometimes left by a flat brush. The long-bristled brushes can be used to produce fluid lines. Because they are easy to control, the short-bristled ones are good for building up an impasto effect, and making short dabs of colour. The smaller sizes are good for detail.

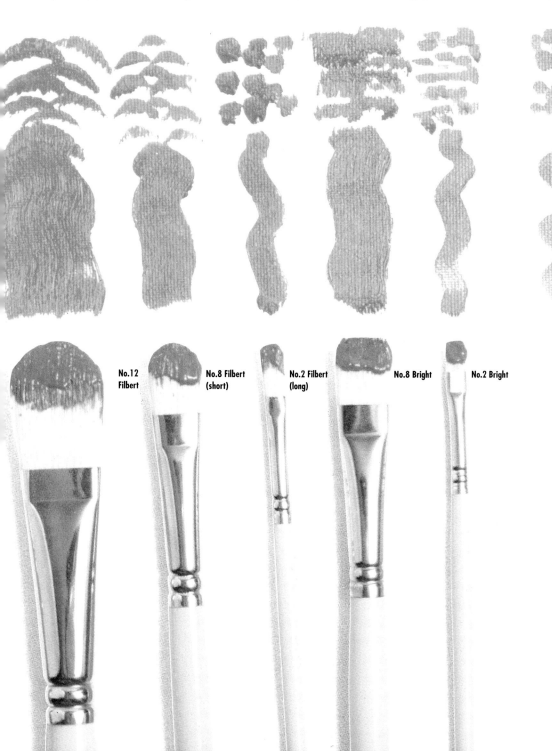

No.12 Filbert · No.8 Filbert (short) · No.2 Filbert (long) · No.8 Bright · No.2 Bright · No.4 Synthetic (round)

Brights – Nos. 8 & 2
Because of the shortness of their bristles, brights are good for building up patches of pure colour in a controlled way.

Synthetic – No.4 round
This brush is good for laying in an area of thin colour, and for details and fine lines.

in each series, with No.12 the largest and No.00, 0 or 1 the smallest.

Beginner's selection

When you start oil painting, bristle brushes are generally more useful than soft ones. Not surprisingly, better quality bristle brushes are more expensive than synthetic substitutes. However, their springiness, versatility and long life make the extra expense worthwhile.

It's far better to buy only three or four really good bristle brushes than a huge selection of poor-quality ones. Choose brushes with hairs that look neat and don't splay out from the ferrule (the metal or plastic case that holds the bristles together). A good selection to start with is a No. 8 round, a No.5 flat and a No.2 filbert or bright. These should cover the basic needs of the beginner, and you can experiment with other styles and sizes later on.

For small-scale or detailed work, you will need a soft brush. Pure sable ones are extremely expensive and unnecessary for the beginner. Moderately priced synthetic soft-hair brushes provide an adequate alternative. A good size to go for is a No.4 or 5 round brush. You may also find ½in or 1in decorators' brushes useful for laying in large areas of colour.

► A medium-sized No. 5 flat is large enough to make broad strokes to describe the bark of this Scots pine, yet small enough to make short dabs of colour for the foliage. The flat edge makes thin, angular lines for the branches.

► A large No. 8 round brush is ideal for laying in large areas of colour. Its flexible bristles allow you to make soft strokes, which, when the brush is angled, create texture for the thick, dense leaves on this cypress.

▲ A smaller brush such as a No.2 round, filbert or bright produces finer, more delicate lines – used here for the small needles on the outer branches of the Norway spruce. The body of the brush, used at an angle, lays in more colour for the denser foliage in the middle.

Palettes and knives for oil

Used by artists for centuries, the palette is still the handiest surface for setting out oil paints. And palette and painting knives are ideal for mixing and applying paint to the canvas.

A palette is a vital part of the oil painter's equipment, enabling him to lay out and mix colours with ease as he stands in front of his canvas or board. Palettes for oil painting come in a variety of sizes, materials and shapes designed to suit the artist's individual requirements. In terms of size alone, the bigger the palette, the easier it is to 'see' the colours. A small palette soon becomes clogged with paint, limiting your ability to mix subtle colour values; a large palette measuring approximately 36 x 46cm (14 x 18in) gives you the chance to space your oils around the rim, and allows plenty of room in the centre for mixing. However it can be quite heavy.

The wooden palette is not as widely used as it once was; its dark brown ground has been seen as a drawback by artists who want to see how their colours look against neutral, white light. Many contemporary artists, however, simply use a palette which approximates to the colour of the support they are working on; this gives them an accurate idea of how the colours will look once applied. So you could choose a wooden palette for working on a toned ground, and a white plastic or disposable paper palette when working on a white ground.

▼ The traditional palette, with its thumbhole and indentation for the fingers and brushes, is supported on the forearm. Dippers for oil and turps can be clipped to the leading edge for convenience.

Traditional palettes are dark, to match the grounds used by painters of the past.

The layout of colours on the palette is a matter of personal preference: some artists arrange them according to the order of the spectrum, others from light to dark.

A

D

▼ Here's a range of palettes of varying qualities.
(A) Disposable paper – perhaps the perfect palettes for
beginners and for those who hate the chore of cleaning
up after each painting session! You can slip a piece of
coloured paper under the top sheet to match your ground.
(B) Mahogany plywood in traditional and square shapes.
Reconstituted mahogany is cheaper than the real thing
and, for most purposes, just as good. Square palettes are
specially designed to be packed away in paint boxes.
(C) Plastic square. The artificial surface is much easier to
clean than wood – ideal for those who like a bare white
palette before every session. (D) Mahogany square. The
most expensive of all palettes, mahogany has a deep
sheen and is lovely to handle.

B

C

B

B

H

F

G

▼(E) Melamine-faced square — another form of plastic palette. (F) Birch plywood — a good lightweight model. (G) Mahogany veneer, traditional shape. This has all the advantages of the pure mahogany palette, but comes very much cheaper. (H) Fibreboard with sepele veneer — a small, lightweight palette with a smooth pure wood surface.

E

G

G

▼ The range of metal palette and painting knives is extremely large, though all have highly flexible steel blades and wooden handles. Palette knives (below) are available in various widths; choose according to palette size and the scale of the task ahead.

The different shapes of painting knives (below right), however, satisfy the demands of a picture for a varied surface texture – some knives may be designed for patting, some for scraping, and so on. But there are no rules in this matter – judge by eye as you go along!

Home-made palettes

You can make your own palette for a fraction of the cost of a studio palette. All you need is an off-cut of marine ply or wood veneer and some simple tools. First, draw a palette outline as smoothly as you can on the wood (don't forget the thumbhole). Second, cut around the outlines with a band or electric saw. Third, sandpaper all the rough edges. And last, apply a coat of varnish to seal the wood and create a smooth working surface.

Palette and painting knives

Palette knives are designed for mixing colours on the palette, scraping palettes clean and scraping wet paint away when making alterations to the picture. They have long, straight, flexible blades with rounded tips: the long edges are ideal for removing wet paint, the tips for picking up and mixing dabs of paint on the palette.

Painting knives, on the other hand, are designed specifically for applying and moving the paint around on the support, particularly when working with thick impastos. Their cranked handles keep your hand clear of the paint surface while you are working, while their blades are springy and angular, and capable of making a great variety of marks. Use the blade tips for fine touches and stippling, the flat undersides for broad strokes, and the edges for making scratchy, linear marks.

Brush cleaner

Some paint-encrusted brushes need to soak in turpentine or white spirit for hours to come clean. During this time the bristles may rest against the bottom of the jar or can and become distorted. One way to avoid this is to use a brush cleaner. These metal containers come in various sizes and have a wide, coiled handle; the brush handle is gripped in the coil, which keeps the brush suspended in the cleaning agent without touching the bottom of the container – ideal for keeping the bristles straight.

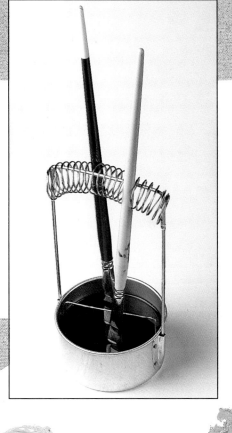

Paper, card and cardboard

The whole matter of oil supports – what to paint on and how to prepare it – can be extremely confusing, especially for the beginner. But a little know-how is all you need to help you choose the right support for your painting.

You can paint on practically anything with oil – wood, paper, hardboard, canvas, even metal – as long as the paint will stick to it. If you're just starting out, though, paper, card and cardboard are excellent first choices. They're cheap, so you can explore the medium without the fear of making a mess of an expensive canvas, and you can use also them for quick sketches. And because they're lightweight, you can store them easily. With paper you can even tape sheets together for a large painting.

But with any oil support, you need to prepare it before you begin to paint.

a more absorbent surface than others. A ground can be toned with a colour, but many artists prefer a white surface (applying a white ground is commonly called 'priming').

Sizing and priming flimsy paper is difficult, so it's best to use at least 140lb paper. A paper with a rough texture supplies a good tooth. With paper and card you size, or size and prime, one side only. Cardboard needs sizing and priming on both sides and on the edges (if it is very thick) to stop it from warping. Thicker cardboard makes a more stable support than paper or thin card.

Sizing and priming

If the oil in oil paint comes into contact with the surface of the support, be it paper, canvas or even wood, it will eventually rot it. To avoid this you apply a thin layer of glue size which shields the support from the paint without reducing the 'tooth' or surface texture too much.

You can use traditional rabbit-skin glue size, available in sheets or crystals which are soaked overnight in water, then gently heated in a double boiler until melted. Glue size also comes in jelly form which you melt down to the right consistency.

You can paint straight on to the sized surface, or give your support a ground. This is another layer which provides a good tooth for the paint to stick to. Grounds have different surfaces, so the one you choose is a matter of preference. For example, some grounds give

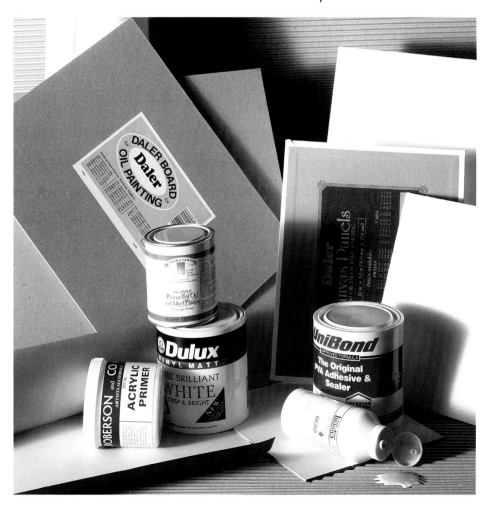

▶ Sizing and priming go hand in hand with paper, card and cardboard supports. Both the supports and the materials needed to prepare them for painting are cheap and easy to use.

The choice is yours

Some people enjoy the process of sizing and priming. Others prefer to buy ready-prepared supports which imitate the surface texture of canvas, in a range from fine to coarse.

Oil sketching paper is available in single sheets or blocks. If you prefer a firm support to work on, go for a block. The sheets are stuck together on four sides and you tear each one off as needed.

Ready-primed canvas boards consist of a piece of canvas mounted on board to give a firm support. They have been treated with a primer so you can paint straight on to them. You can buy them from art shops in a variety of surface textures and a good range of standard sizes.

If you prefer the luxury of a ready-prepared support, be prepared for the expense – they are quite costly compared with unprepared surfaces.

Choosing a primer

You can prepare oil supports with any one of a variety of primers. Some are specially made for oil painting, but others are made up from ordinary household paint.

PVA/Emulsion is a quick-drying primer which you make by mixing roughly equal measures of PVA and ordinary household emulsion paint. Dilute it with water to make a solution that has the consistency of single cream. There's no need to size the paper or card before applying it.

Acrylic primer is simply an acrylic medium mixed with white acrylic paint. It can be used as a ground for acrylic or oil paints. Apply it directly to the support without using size, or mix in a little coloured acrylic paint for a tinted ground. Acrylic medium by itself dries transparent, so if you apply it to cardboard, you retain the colour, giving you a warm middle tone to work on.

Oil primer is available from artists' suppliers, but a good-quality, household, oil-based undercoat paint does just as well. It takes longer to dry between coats than acrylic primer or emulsion glaze but some people prefer it because it makes a more durable ground. Mix in some oil paint for a tinted ground.

Gesso is only suitable for cardboard, not paper, because it is inflexible and tends to crack on a bendy support. Made from fine chalk and rabbit-skin glue size, it provides a very fine smooth surface for painting on. Gesso is available from art shops.

Do's and dont's

There are a few basic rules which are important to remember, whether you are using a size or a primer.

1 Apply several *thin* coats of primer or glue size. A thin coat is supple and pliable while a thick coat is likely to crack and may even flake off the canvas.

2 Make sure the entire surface is evenly covered, but don't go back over your brushstrokes or the coat of size or primer will be too thick.

3 Let each coat dry thoroughly before applying the next. Emulsion and acrylic primers dry faster than oil primers. Test by touching the surface lightly with your finger – if the primer feels tacky, it isn't dry.

YOU WILL NEED

- ☐ A sheet of fine 20 x 16in oil paper
- ☐ A 4B graphite stick
- ☐ Palette
- ☐ Turps and dipper
- ☐ Masking tape
- ☐ White spirit
- ☐ Three brushes: a No.8 flat, a No.4 filbert and a 1in flat decorators' brush
- ☐ Cleaning rag
- ☐ Nine oil colours: cadmium red, chrome orange, titanium white, cadmium red deep, cadmium yellow, raw umber, cerulean blue, French ultramarine, yellow ochre

---

Playing on the beach

▶ **The set-up** Two red buckets and a blue spade, with a scatter of pretty shells, made a bright, cheerful grouping which caught our artist's eye and provided the inspiration for this seaside painting.

Our artist chose oil paper for speed. Even the fine textured grades have enough tooth to hold oil paint well – this tooth actually helps to remove or 'pull' the paint from the brush.

He used the *alla prima* approach, painting straight on to the paper with no underpainting or priming – and with just one layer of paint. He used bold brushstrokes, keeping his paint really buttery by mixing it with only tiny amounts of turps, and covered the surface quickly, starting with the main elements – buckets, spade, shells and sandcastles and finishing with the large area of sandy beach in the background.

Tip

Plan your palette
You'll find mixing colours much easier if you plan your palette in advance. Group similar

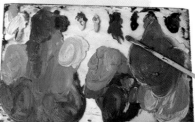

colours together and keep similar mixes next to each other on the palette. Also, try to leave a little of each mix you use in case you need more of it.

▶ **1** Tape your paper securely to the drawing board with masking tape, then sketch in the main outlines of the composition with the 4B graphite stick.
Pour some turps into your dipper and squeeze out a little of each colour on to your palette.

◀ **2** With the No.8 flat brush, mix some cadmium red deep with just a touch of ultramarine. Dilute the mix with a little turps and use to paint the inside of the top bucket. Add cadmium red to lighten the mix for the outside rim. Carry on with the same mix to block in the whole of this bucket, and also the bottom bucket. Keep the paint buttery by using only small amounts of turps.
Lighten the mixture with tiny blobs of cadmium yellow and titanium white to make a slightly paler red for the rim of the second bucket (see inset below). Notice how the artist has used his darkest tones for the inside of both buckets.

▶ **3** Lighten the mix again with titanium white to make a light pink and, using the No.4 filbert brush, paint the outside lip of the top bucket. Add a touch of cadmium yellow and paint in the light area under the bucket rim.

Clean your brush with white spirit, then mix some cerulean blue with a little titanium white and block in the blade of the spade. For the shadows on the blade, mix cerulean blue with a touch of raw umber.

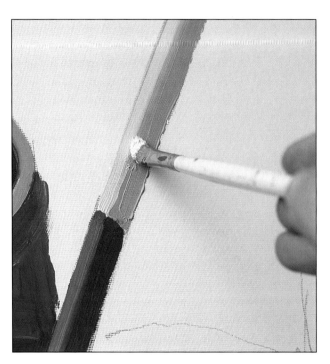

▲ **4** Clean your No.4 brush again and mix titanium white, yellow ochre, raw umber and a touch of the blue you already have on the palette to make a grey-blue for the right hand side of the spade handle. Paint this in, then lighten the mix with a little titanium white for the lighter, left hand side of the handle. Mix up a tiny amount of titanium white and yellow ochre and paint in a thin line down the centre of the handle between the darker and lighter grey tones.

Tip

Primer points
You can use oil paints over an acrylic primer, but NEVER paint with acrylic over an oil primer. If you are preparing several different kinds of ground in one go, label the back of each support to ensure you don't put acrylic over an oil primer by mistake.

▶ **5** Go back to the pinky red mix on your palette and mix in some yellow ochre to make a darker red for the shells inside the bottom bucket. Paint one or two shells in this colour, then darken the mix with a touch of the blue on your palette. Use this for the darker areas where the red of the bucket casts a stronger shadow on the shells.

Stand back from time to time and squint at your painting to assess the various tones you are introducing.

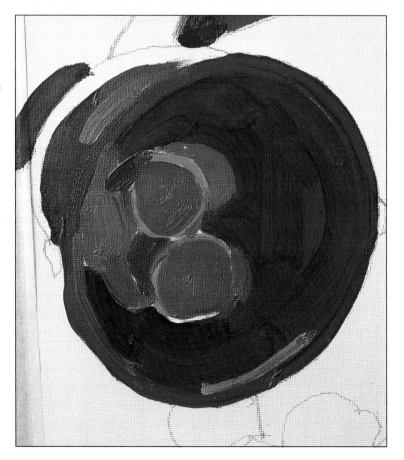

◄ 6 Add a touch of chrome orange to the mix you used for the light grey of the spade handle to make a creamy, light yellow. Paint in the handle of the bottom bucket with the No.4 filbert. Then mix some titanium white into the darker grey shade used on the spade handle and paint in the right hand side of the handle of the top bucket. The left hand side of this handle is left white – the white of the paper itself.

Now turn your attention to the shells. Mix the grey you just used with a touch of blue from your palette. Use this to paint in the bluer shells on the right. Add a touch of red from the palette to make a pink for the shells on the left.

Make up a series of tints for the shells, using raw umber, then a touch of darker blue from the palette or a touch of pinky red to make lighter and darker greys and mushroomy pinks. Use the tip of the No.4 brush to paint in the streaks on the shells. Add titanium white to the mixes for the lighter areas inside the shells.

► 7 Now for the background sand. Mix yellow ochre and white to make a light sandy colour, then darken some of it by adding raw umber, cadmium red and cerulean blue. With the No.4 filbert, dab touches of these two mixes here and there on the bottom two-thirds of the background area (the top third of your painting will be lighter and contain less detail to give the impression of receding into the distance). The small dabbing brushstrokes give depth and texture.

Use the darker mix for the shadows on the two sandcastles, and the lighter mix for the lighter parts – try to get a gradation of tones from light to dark here to give the sandcastles a rounded shape.

8 Clean your palette by scraping off the remains of the paint, then wipe down with a rag dipped in white spirit. You now want a light ochre, unadulterated by any other colour, for the rest of the sand.

Mix some white and yellow ochre – make it quite a pale creamy yellow to bring out the contrast with the darker touches of ochre paint already on the paper. Add a touch of chrome orange to warm the colour slightly, and then more yellow ochre and titanium white so the paint is buttery. Make a lot of this mixture so you have enough to cover the whole area now remaining.

◄ 9 With your No.8 flat brush, paint in the sandy background, starting at the bottom of the picture. Cut in carefully around the shells, the bottom bucket and the spade blade, correcting their shapes as necessary with your ochre mix. Darken the sand area around the handle of the bottom bucket or the two colours will be too similar.

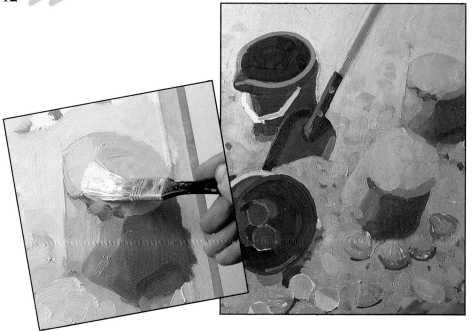

◄ 10 Make a lighter ochre colour by adding some white to your existing mix. Change to the decorators' brush and block in all the sand area in the top third of the picture. Add some of this lighter colour to the top of both the sandcastles and on their left hand edges (see inset left).

Use the No.4 filbert brush to paint around the spade and between the top bucket and its handle, taking care to leave the white half of this handle clear and clean. Finally, use the ochre mix to touch in the bit of yellow handle on the right hand side of the bottom bucket, and the two nail heads on the spade handle.

Notice how your eye is now automatically drawn to the bottom half of the picture, where there's more detail and the sand tones are darker. The lighter areas of sand at the top recede into the distance.

▲ 11 To give a little more detail to the shells in the foreground, draw in a few lines on top of them with your 4B graphite stick. Notice how the tooth of the paper shows through the pencil marks, giving texture to the shells. This last touch strengthens the foreground and balances the strong reds and blues of buckets and spade.

► 12 The final image is bright and cheerful, with a really bold use of primary colours. The fine texture of the oil paper reflects the smooth, grainy feeling of sand, adding to the lively summertime mood.

PART 2

Creative Techniques

Fat over lean

Find out how to build up layers of oil paint to create a rich, lustrous and long-lasting surface to your paintings.

Depending on how much you dilute it or how thinly you apply it, oil paint can be transparent or opaque. Transparent applications, always thin, are called glazes. You can put these directly on to the canvas or over thin layers of opaque colour, or use them over the top of thickly applied paint to modify the colour beneath. By building up glazes one on the other you create a surface with great depth and luminosity, giving your painting an 'inner light'.

You can apply the paint opaquely in thin washes or patches of colour, or in thick creamy passages which retain the mark of brush, knife, finger or rag.

▼ **Here every inch is packed with lively paintwork. The orange drawing shows through and catches the eye. Cool glazes on the cut surfaces of the melons and apples suggest moistness and provide areas of calm relief among the vibrant reds, oranges, blues and green.**
Detail of 'Melons and red apples' by Moira Huntly, 19 x 24in

Mixing paint

1 Palette knife; **2** Turps substitute; **3** Dipper with pure turps and linseed oil; **4** Dipper with pure turps; **5** Mixing area; **6** Clean rag

Use a palette knife to transfer paint to the mixing area and then mix the colours together with the knife.

Add turps and/or linseed oil, using a clean brush, and mix with the brush. Use *only* pure turps to thin your paint. Use turps substitute to clean your brushes between colours.

As your painting progresses, typical percentages of turps to oil might be: 100; 75/25; 50/50; 40/60.

The traditional approach

In classical oil painting the picture is built up in layers. Since oil paint dries slowly, the surface has to dry before you apply a new layer, so your progress is steady and considered. If the layers are especially thick it could take weeks or even months to complete a painting.

Artists using oils often start by drawing in the image with charcoal or thinned paint, or blocking it in as an underpainting using paint thinned with turpentine. The underpainting could be a monochrome 'tonal' underpainting, or you could lay in the broad areas of colour. The painting is then developed layer upon layer with glazes, opaque washes or even thickly applied impasto.

When working in this traditional way it's important to work 'fat over lean'. 'Fat' describes paint used straight from the tube, or paint to which extra linseed oil has been added. This makes the paint more fluid when wet and flexible when dry. 'Lean' paint has little or no extra oil and is thinned with turps. It dries quicker than fat paint and can soon be overpainted. The idea is to start with lean paint, reducing the turps as the painting progresses and adding linseed oil to the top layers – which need to flex. This prevents cracking and is important with canvas – which is itself flexible.

In the following demonstration the artist chose to use canvas board. The advantage of this is that, unlike canvas, it doesn't need stretching.

Wooden spoons in a jug

The group is quite a simple one – and at first glance just a few wooden spoons in a jug. But look at the subject with a painter's eye. The utensils sprout energetically from the jug like flowers from a vase, providing an array of shapes and subtle tones. You may think wood is simply brown but look carefully and you'll see a host of neutral greys, and warm and cool browns too – all contrasting with the cooler blues in the pottery jug.

▶ **The set-up**

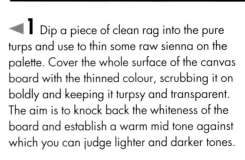

◀ **1** Dip a piece of clean rag into the pure turps and use to thin some raw sienna on the palette. Cover the whole surface of the canvas board with the thinned colour, scrubbing it on boldly and keeping it turpsy and transparent. The aim is to knock back the whiteness of the board and establish a warm mid tone against which you can judge lighter and darker tones.

◄2 Put some raw sienna into the middle of the palette with the palette knife. Thin it by adding a little turps with a clean No. 4 round brush and use it to block in the broad forms of the utensils. Look at the spaces between the utensils and the shapes they make against the background. Check these in your painting. If your drawing goes wrong, wipe off the paint with a rag and correct it.

Use the same brush to lay in the jug with some turpsy white paint. Then lighten some cobalt blue and put in the jug handle, some shadow on the side of the jug – just to give a hint of form – and an outline round the base. Then let the surface dry.

3 Lighten some Payne's gray with white, then thin it with turps using a No. 5 flat brush. Lay in the top of the black tablecloth. For the time being, use a single horizontal line to indicate the table edge.

◄4 Lay in the darker front of the cloth with some Payne's gray and turps. Here the artist works back over the right side of the table top to make it darker. This decision was made after checking how the light fell on the table. Check how the light is falling on your group and make similar adjustments where necessary.

▼5 Make a mix of 75/25 turps/linseed oil in a dipper. Nick a little white with the palette knife and put it in the mixing area. Add some of the turps/oil mix with the round No. 4 brush then use the mix to overpaint the background in bold strokes.

As you're painting in the background you're defining the edges of the utensils at the same time, so avoid over-trimming the outlines. See how the warm underpainting modifies the white.

◄6 Start to overpaint the utensils, using the same mix of turps and oil and the same brush. Screw up your eyes and look at the tones in your group.

Here the artist used a mix of yellow ochre and cobalt blue to make a warm green for the spatula. The spoon at the side of the jug is a more ochre version of the same mix. The spoon at the front is darker in tone, but actually much warmer and has been blocked in with a mix of raw sienna and cadmium red.

7 Keep the same colours working throughout. You can see here that the artist repeated versions of the ochre-green and raw sienna in several places. These are overpainted later but for the moment they draw the group together.

When you come to the jug remember that it is a cylinder. Don't dive straight in and paint the hoops. Instead describe its form first – lighten some ochre-green, add a little cobalt and use vertical strokes to work darker tones into the jug's body and handle.

8 Add some linseed oil to the turps/oil dipper so that the mix is roughly 50/50. Mix up some pale cobalt blue and use the No. 2 round brush to put the hoops on the jug. Mixing takes place with paint already on the canvas, but this helps to make the blue less intense. The artist has also added some of the ochre used for the utensils.

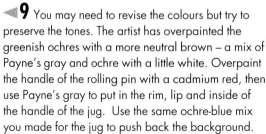

9 You may need to revise the colours but try to preserve the tones. The artist has overpainted the greenish ochres with a more neutral brown – a mix of Payne's gray and ochre with a little white. Overpaint the handle of the rolling pin with a cadmium red, then use Payne's gray to put in the rim, lip and inside of the handle of the jug. Use the same ochre-blue mix you made for the jug to push back the background.

◄**10** So far you have kept the edges indefinite – a good policy because it helps your eye to rove across the surface, encouraging you to make adjustments as you go. Now start tightening the painting a little. Scratch out the ovals and curves of the spoons with the end of a brush.

▼**11** Still keeping a 50/50 mix of turps and oil, and your No. 2 flat brush, use lightened yellow ochre to render the light areas of wood and describe the curved forms more fully.

With your No. 5 flat brush, define the lip of the jug by revisiting the background with a bit of white. While you're at it, put a bit of sparkle back into the body and handle of the jug with touches of white.

◄**12** Step back from your painting and look at how the whole is working. Here you can see that, compared with step 9, the utensils are really starting to take form. Notice how the painting is still quite loose. This is a good stage at which to let the painting dry.

SOLVE IT

Removing surplus oil
A wet oily surface can be difficult to paint over. If you haven't time to let it dry, blot off the surplus paint using a piece of absorbent paper — such as newspaper. (This technique is known as 'tonking' after Henry Tonks, the Professor of Painting at the Slade School who invented it.) Lay the paper over the surplus paint and rub over it lightly with the tips of your fingers to make sure that it is in contact with the paint. Peel off the paper carefully.

◀**13** Start to tighten the painting. Make a 40/60 mix of turps and oil, and with your No. 2 flat brush make subtle adjustments by glazing over existing colours. You may need to tone down some of the light ochres with darker, cooler browns and greys, for example.

Never be afraid to make fairly large changes if you can see they will improve your painting. Here the artist simplifies the whole surface of the spatula with an oily but opaque layer of yellow ochre and Payne's gray with a little white.

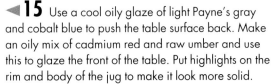

▲**14** Really let yourself go on those spoons! Using some darker browns, scoop out the hollows with shadow and put a bit of warm reflected colour on to the wood. Red acts as a focal point at the front of the group and, used sparingly on the spoon behind, leads the eye up through the painting to the handle of the rolling pin.

◀**15** Use a cool oily glaze of light Payne's gray and cobalt blue to push the table surface back. Make an oily mix of cadmium red and raw umber and use this to glaze the front of the table. Put highlights on the rim and body of the jug to make it look more solid.

The predominant colours might be various browns but notice how they make the blues, reds and ochres work even harder, really bringing your painting to life!

Making your mark

With oils, more than any other paint, your brushstrokes are as much a vehicle for expression as the colour and composition. Learn to exploit and develop the character of your brushstrokes.

Oil paint has a wonderful tactile quality and is unique in the way it takes on the character of the brushstrokes. Whether you apply oils energetically with bold, swirling rhythms (like van Gogh) or calmly in smooth, carefully measured strokes, this character remains apparent in your finished painting. The strokes are imprinted into the paint – they create a texture – and can say as much about you and your feelings towards your subject as they can about the subject itself.

The brushstrokes you can make are as varied as your imagination. You might create a highly ordered – patterned – surface using strokes of a similar size and direction, or go for an entirely random texture. Common sense should always prevail, though. If you want broad brushstrokes,

use a broad brush. If you want a flat (not rounded) end to the stroke, use a brush with a flat end – such as a flat or bright. The right brush enables you to make a stroke which stands on its own – giving your painting a more spontaneous feel. If you find yourself fiddling about, your brush is probably too small.

The best way to develop your brushstrokes is not by practising them in isolation but by making paintings and experimenting. Not everyone will use the same type of strokes for a subject – but this doesn't matter at all. In the demonstration that follows, feel free to use an entirely different set of brushstrokes from our artist if you wish.

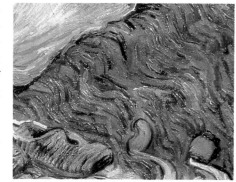

◄▲ **Van Gogh used bold brushstrokes to show form and movement in his paintings. Look at the detail of the hay under the sleeping figures (above). The strongly directional brushstrokes suggest comfortable ripples in the straw and reveal every strand. Notice that even on the shoes and the man's feet, the artist reveals form with the direction of his brushstrokes – this time with a finer brush.**
'Noon after millet' by Vincent van Gogh, oil on canvas, 73 x 91in

Trees on the green

▲ **The set-up** Choose a subject with plenty of scope for creative brushwork. Horse chestnut trees on Hadley Green at Barnet in Hertfordshire provided the inspiration for our artist. He used two photo references, combining them to make the composition more effective. The main subjects are the house and surrounding trees but our artist felt his composition would be improved by a strong vertical on the right. He used a photo of a tree from another part of Hadley Green.

◄ **1** Loosely sketch in the main forms with a turpsy mix of blue and violet. (You might find it easier to paint over a scant charcoal sketch.) A light wipe over with a clean, dry cotton rag helps the paint dry quicker and makes your underpainting less obtrusive.

With a mix of cobalt blue and Winsor violet and the No.5 filbert, paint the darkest tones – such as those on the trunks under the canopies. Then add some Venetian red to your mix to make a rich dark brown and, using the same brush, paint in the next darkest tones – as our artist is doing here.

▶ **2** Now look for the lightest tones – here they're in the sky. Mix up some white and cerulean blue and paint the sky with your No.8 flat.

Avoid vertical and/or horizontal strokes of the sort you'd use for painting your front door! Instead, hold your brush close to the head and use rolling strokes to work life into the paint.

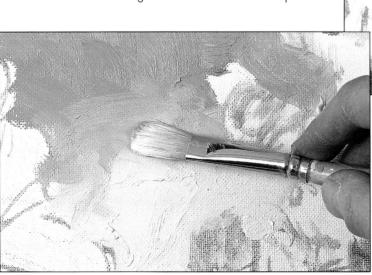

◄ **3** Even cloudless skies are rarely one shade of blue. Most have other colours – such as pale greys and violets – and the blue is often less intense than it first appears. Add a hint of red to white to make a slightly off-white for areas of cloud on the horizon. Use the No.7 filbert to push the paint between the trees and clumps of leaves. Then add a hint of violet to your mix and paint the change between the clouds and sky, keeping the surface lively.

4 While you've still got some white and red mixed, add a touch of Winsor yellow and, using the same brush, paint in the path.

◀ **5** Our artist stressed the importance of 'keying-in' the tones – that is, tracking logically around the painting, assessing the tones of one form against another.

Having painted the sky, assess the tones of the trees against it. Make a white/cerulean/violet mix, aiming for a violet-grey mid-tone. Then, using the No.8 flat, paint in the lighter foliage as it's seen against the sky.

▶ **6** Look carefully at your own subject and try to follow this mid-tone through the trees, stopping when you reach denser, darker banks of shadow, or lighter, brightly coloured bursts of foliage. As you approach warmer areas, drop in just a touch of red to your mix.

Never be afraid to edit or add if it improves your painting. Our artist invented a man and dog to help lead your eye in.

▼ **7** Now look for the rich russet shadows under, around and between the sunlit clusters of leaves. Paint these with a mix of white, cerulean, violet and red. Use the same brush. Don't worry about making a fool of yourself – be bold!

Bring depth to your painting by putting cooler colours under the trees in the middleground. Try mixes of green oxide, permanent green, cobalt blue and white for the greens and blue-greens. Mix white and violet for the shadows on the path and tree trunk. (You might find a smaller brush – such as the No.5 flat – useful here.)

▶ **8** Here you can see how our artist used blues, greens and violets to join the darks to the light areas (such as the path and sunlit foliage in the trees). Notice how the shadows are not flat and lifeless but loosely painted and entertaining, and how the trees billow from the landscape like plumes of smoke.

9 (If, at this stage, your palette has become muddy, clean it with white spirit before starting on the lighter colours.)

Model the lighter foliage with a mix of red, violet, yellow and white using the No.7 filbert and No.8 flat brushes. Keep the colours warm but fairly subdued. If you want an even richer, warmer colour, add more red and yellow. (Our artist used a mix like this for the base of the foliage here.)

10 Leave the lightest areas in the trees until last (you can see from the white patches of canvas where our artist intends to put them). Now move on to the tree in the foreground, on the right.

11 This tree is closer to the picture plane. So the contrast between the lights and darks in its foliage is greater and its texture more pronounced. Enjoy yourself with expressive brushstrokes to capture this in your painting. Using the No.8 flat brush, build up to the lightest tints – mixes of red, yellow and white. Here and there you might have to revert to a dark brown – such as the russet you made in step 7 – for shadows under the bright sprays of foliage.

12 To make the sprays appear to come out towards you, place shadows carefully under the sprays, and add highlights where the leaves appear to be nearest to you. Our artist used short, swirling brushstrokes to do two jobs: to make the tree look solid and to increase the painting's entertainment value by making its surface exciting.

13 Now you've worked the lightest tones into the nearest tree, return to the trees on the left. Track through with the same colours but use smaller brushes – such as the No.5 flat and filbert. These trees are farther away, so the texture in their canopies appears less pronounced. Use only light pressure (so just the tip of the brush strokes the surface) and blend the colours together to give the foliage a mellow feel.

14 Now make a light mix of chrome green, permanent green, yellow and a touch of white for the strip of sunlit grass. (Don't add too much white or your green will appear too washed out.)

Work boldly with the No.8 flat brush to keep the paint lively. Once you've got a feel for the general tone of this green strip, modulate the colours.

15 Touches of yellowy green – particularly at the front of the strip – create the impression of sunlight on the grass. Cooler (bluer) greens recede to meet the blues and violets under the trees. You might try breaking the green strip with a patch of the same colour you used for the path.

SOLVE IT

Using a mahlstick

To complete his painting, our artist straightened the ridge on the roof of the house. This required a steady hand, but since this feature was surrounded entirely by wet paint, he used a mahlstick (a stick, generally with

a ball on one end, used to steady the artist's hand). In this case, his mahlstick was a length of broom handle.

◄ **16** Paint the tree trunk with a mix of white, red and a touch of violet. Then add a few final touches. These are a matter of personal choice, and though they are only superficial, they can still affect the mood of the painting – as you can see from our artist's completed work.

▼ **17** He used the No.2 flat to neaten the edges of the house. Then he added texture to the grass by stroking into the paint with the tip of the No.6 brush and yellow paint straight from the tube. These small strokes contrast well with the much broader swirling strokes in the trees.

It's worth noting that although the subject is fairly simple and static, the sheer variety of brushstrokes makes it satisfying and entertaining to the eye.

Scumbling with oil paint

The word scumbling is rather strange, but the technique itself couldn't be simpler – it's a straightforward way of introducing texture and broken colour effects into your paintings.

To achieve a *textural* scumbling you drag thick paint lightly across the picture surface so that patches of the underlying colour show through the scumbled paint.

You can do this thick scumbling with a brush or painting knife, and it works on any toothy surface – including canvas, oil paper and paint itself. The paint must be as thick as possible, not diluted with turpentine. Good-quality paints are best because they contain less oil and have a stiffer consistency.

The alternative means of scumbling is effectively the reverse of a glaze – it is a film of paint that can be thin or creamy as long as it's also opaque or semi-opaque. With a semi-opaque scumble you modify rather than obliterate the colour beneath.

Another way of avoiding a complete cover like this is to apply the scumble with a dry brush, so you allow flecks or larger areas of the underlying colour to show through.

In the demonstration overleaf we show you textural scumbling. Scumbling with a thin film is covered in the next chapter.

▼ In this charming painting of a lavender field in France, the artist has achieved an exciting surface texture by scumbling paint on with fingers, brushes and painting knives.
'Lavender in Provence' by Madge Bright, oil on canvas, 25 x 36in

Scumbling with a painting knife and with a brush

1 A knife produces thick wedges of uneven paint that contrast with the thinner undercolour. Scoop up some paint on the underside of the knife and scrape it lightly across the surface, with the edge of the blade tilted.

2 For more regular texture, load a large flat bristle brush with undiluted paint and drag this lightly across the canvas. Hold the brush very close to the canvas, painting with the flattened side of the bristle head.

Ducks on walkabout

Scumbling works best on a textured surface, so used primed canvas or cotton duck for this painting. Buy a ready-to-use stretched canvas or simply use a length of primed canvas and stick it down on a rigid board with masking tape.

The initial drawing is crucial, so take time getting this right. You'll find it helpful to make a few quick sketches of the subject first, then copy one on to the canvas. Keep the drawing as simple as possible – too much drawn detail is a waste of time because it will get covered up as soon as you start to paint.

▲ **1** Use charcoal for the initial drawing, giving the ducks a single, confident outline. For the background, a few accurate lines are enough to establish the position of the bridge and buildings.

◀ **2** By making a textured underpainting in neutral acrylic or alkyd paint you lessen the drying time and can scumble over it in oil paint almost immediately without smudging the painted outline. For the outline, use a No.0 round brush and a mixture of phthalo blue and burnt sienna – this produces a very dark tone which is less stark than black.

▶ **3** While the outline is drying, squeeze out your oil colours on to the palette – burnt sienna, carmine alizarin, terra rosa, Naples yellow, French ultramarine, olive green, cadmium yellow, cadmium red and white.

Using the No.12 flat brush, apply a loose wash mixture of terra rosa, carmine alizarin and burnt sienna across the ground and sky. Don't worry about drips and runs – these quickly become integrated into the picture.

◀ **4** For the river, use the 2in flat brush to apply a thin wash of French ultramarine in short, vertical strokes. Paint over the outline of the ducks, but leave a few patches of white on the lightest parts of the birds.

◀ **5** The blue and reddish brown washes look more natural if you allow them to overlap in places. Paint the shadows cast by the ducks and those on the ducks themselves in a darker tone of the blue wash colour.

► **6** For the pale background areas, mix a little white and Naples yellow with the blue and brownish red already used in the painting. Bring the ducks to life by painting the light tones in pale blue with your No.10 flat brush.

▼ **7** Paint the black duck with the No.4 flat brush. Real black would be too dominant, so use a mixture of olive green, French ultramarine and a little carmine alizarin.

◄ **8** It's almost time to start adding texture – time to start scumbling the ducks! But first you need to re-establish the duck outlines, which have become lost under washes of colour. Do this with your No.0 brush and the acrylic or alkyd paint.

◀**9** For the first layer of scumbled colour, dip the No.10 brush into thick white paint – don't add any turps – and drag the loaded brush lightly across the canvas inside the outlines of the ducks. The pressure should be light enough to allow patches of undercolour to show through the thick paint.

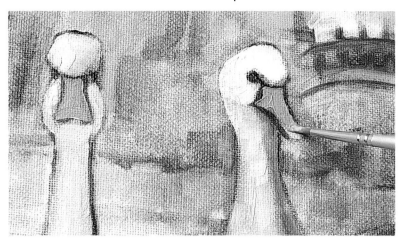

▲**10** For the beaks and feet, mix a bright orange from cadmium yellow and cadmium red and apply this with your No.4 flat brush.

Tip

Keep it dry
When you are scumbling in this textural way, keep your paint thick but dry – use very little turps (preferably none at all, in fact).
Another point to bear in mind when you start is that scumbling works best on a textured surface.
Don't forget to use your fingers, either – they're great tools for scumbling.

◀**11** Lighten the shadows underneath the ducks with a light scumble of white and French ultramarine. For the shadows on the feet, use the dark tone – olive green, French ultramarine and a little alizarin carmine – painting them in with the No.0 brush.

DID YOU KNOW?

Cloisonné

Our artist has outlined her ducks in a fairly dark line. This is known as cloisonné, and is a technique taken from a style of jewellery in which outlines created by thin wire are filled in with brightly coloured enamel. The dark outlines highlight the bright colours inside. The French artist Paul Gauguin did many paintings in this style.

▲ **12** You can create the illusion of distance by applying a pale blue scumble across the entire background area. Do this with the No.10 brush, held flat against the canvas, and apply the stiff colour in short vertical strokes to indicate the geometric, upright buildings.

◄ **13** Lighten the very pale background areas a bit more by cross-scumbling – pulling the brush horizontally across the previous vertical strokes. Your scumble should be light enough to allow the shapes of the buildings to show through.

► **14** Redefine the light background tones and highlights in white using your No.4 flat brush.

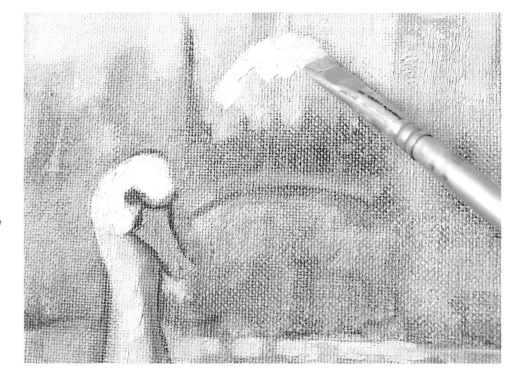

▲ 15 The painting is almost complete, and it's time to stand back and take a critical look at the picture so far. Notice how the white ducks have become too similar in tone and texture to the background. They need to be brightened and strengthened.

▶ 16 A painting knife is useful here. Use it to scumble a thick layer of white on to the ducks. Use the direction of the strokes to describe the curved forms of the birds.

▶ **17** Take care not to scumble a complete layer of white all over the ducks. Retain some shadows on the birds by allowing a few areas of darker underpainting to show through. These dark patches, and the shaded parts of the necks and abdomens, make the birds look solid and real.

▼ **18** In the finished picture the scumbled areas of white on the ducks – with the darker colours showing through – give zest and life to what could otherwise have been areas of dead colour. The bright beaks and feet contrast well with the white, while the gentle blues and earth colours of the background give a sense of hazy distance.

Scumbling and glazing

Scumbling and glazing will help you capture the shifting, shimmering light of a landscape. Underlying colours appear to glow through the upper layers, creating a wonderful translucency.

The previous demonstration showed you how to scumble with thick paint. But you can also use thin paint for scumbling, provided it's fairly opaque. As with thick paint, you apply the colour unevenly so the colours underneath can show through.

Some colours are more opaque than others, but in general, if you thin a colour with plenty of turps it becomes transparent. Then you have a glaze, which you can apply thinly over the colours on the canvas, building up the layers so that each colour shimmers through the next. White is a highly opaque colour, so if you want to scumble rather than glaze, adding a little white to the colour will help. In the demonstration overleaf our artist painted a stormy sky off the coast of Ireland using glazes and scumbles to capture the nebulous quality of the scene. You should note that this painting takes several days to complete.

▼ A mixture of scumbles, glazes and loosely dragged brushstrokes give the surface of this painting a lively texture. Notice how the artist repeats colours in different parts of the painting for a unifying effect, such as the violet in the sky and on the boat hulls, for example.
'Bosham' by John Denahy, oil on canvas, 12½ x 15in

Rising storm

▶1 Our artist used sketches he'd made on site in Ireland as the basis of this painting. Use his finished painting as your reference or work from a sketch or photo of your own.

Using the No.6 round brush and cobalt violet thinned with turps, sketch in the main elements of your composition – the horizon, the hills in the distance and the beach. Notice how our artist holds his brush loosely, his hand well down the handle to give plenty of wrist movement.

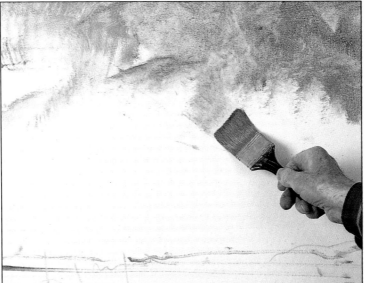

◀2 One by one, dip into Rembrandt blue, rose madder and brown madder alizarin with the 2½in decorators' brush, thinning each colour with plenty of turps so that it is quite watery. Liberally and somewhat randomly apply each colour to the upper sky, blending them where they meet.

▶3 Working down to the horizon, continue laying in the colours of the sky, adding a mix of turquoise and titanium white for the bluest areas and the sea. Switch to the 1½in decorators' brush to vary the brushstrokes.

Our artist really scrubs the paint into the weave of the canvas, working the brush in several directions to give the sky energy and movement.

▶ **4** Now apply some of this blue mix, lightened with white, to the sky – use your metal wallpaper scraper for this to create subtle texture. This unconventional tool has a wide, flexible blade, perfect for applying large blocks of colour. Where necessary you can use the edge of the blade to scrape away excess paint.

Tip

Soft paper

Tonking (removing excess oil by pressing over the painting with paper) is usually done with newspaper, but you can use all sorts of absorbent papers – either whatever you have to hand, or a paper which gives a particular finish. Our artist used ordinary soft toilet paper.

◀ **5** Indicate the beach with a mix of brilliant yellow deep, titanium white and yellow raw ochre using the 1½in decorators' brush. Then add a little of the same mix to the sky to link it to the landscape.

With the basic colours loosely washed in, check your composition – now is the time to make adjustments. This underpainting also provides a foundation for further layers of colour, and it kills the white of the canvas, which can be rather intimidating.

▶ **6** Map in the distant hills with emerald green. Now plot one or two verticals to offset the main horizontals of the composition. Use the scraper to do this, dipping into brown madder alizarin, Rembrandt blue and cobalt violet simultaneously without mixing them, then press the scraper on to the canvas. Soften the lines by tonking (see Tip, above right).

Tip

Using a fan

A sable fan brush is the perfect shape for painting the soft edges of clouds. Press the head of the brush against the support so the hairs splay out a little, and dab the paint on with small movements of the brush.

◄7 Go over the sky in the same colours as before, this time using the paint slightly thicker in a half-and-half mix with alkyd medium and turps. (The alkyd medium increases transparency and reduces brushmarks.) Use a mix of bluish grey and cobalt violet to go over the distant hills.

Now paint the marshland in the distance with a mix of emerald green, titanium white and brilliant yellow deep, using the scraper to apply the colour with broken, ragged strokes.

►8 Switching between your 1½in decorators' brush, No.6 sable fan and No.6 filbert to invigorate the sky, work on the dramatic storm clouds. Use a mix of bluish grey, brown madder alizarin, Prussian blue and purple rose for the brooding cloud at the top right.

Now put in some grey clouds on the bottom left with a mix of bluish grey tinged with white, and add a dash of emerald green to the centre to reflect the landscape. For the lighter area on the left, use King's blue and titanium white.

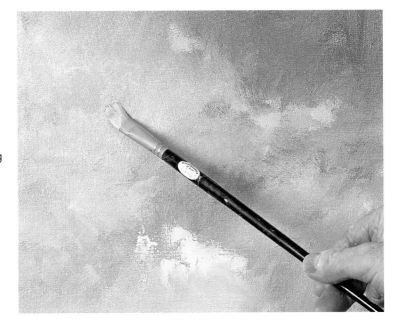

►9 Move on to the foreground, adding details with the same colours as before.

Now our artist stood back to assess the overall effect and decided to lighten the sky with more pale grey clouds. For these he used bluish grey and a little titanium white, applied with the sable fan. Leave the painting to dry otherwise the next paint layers will blend into these first colours.

◀**10** Returning to the dry painting with a fresh eye, our artist decided that the large storm cloud needed enriching, so he brushed over it with the 1½in decorators' brush, and a transparent glaze of Talens red deep thinned with alkyd medium and turps.

▶**11** Glaze over the clouds below the storm cloud with purple rose (a transparent colour), then rub it in with a cotton rag to leave a soft, smooth stain of colour with no brushmarks. These thin scumbles and glazes capture the luminosity of the sky.

▼**12** Still working on the sky, add a spark of high-key colour near the horizon with the No.6 fan. Our artist used a mix of turquoise and white. It's a truly gorgeous colour, but be careful not to overuse it or its impact will be lost.

► **13** Return to the sea and deepen the tones in the foremost strip of water with mixtures of ultramarine deep, cobalt violet and touches of turquoise blue and white, using your large decorators' brush. This helps to bring the area forward.

▼ **14** For the final touch, change to your filbert brush and add short dashes of colour to suggest grasses. Use yellow and the various mixes you made for the sky.

In the finished painting you can see how the lively quality of the paint contributes to the overall impression of a brooding storm.

Broken-colour effects

The term 'broken colour' encompasses techniques such as drybrushing, glazing and scumbling, but it's also used to describe a method of applying small strokes of colour which mix optically.

The great landscape artist John Constable (1776-1837) noted that 'no two days are alike, nor even two hours; neither were there ever two leaves of a tree alike since the creation of the world'. So he set about capturing this individuality and the changes of light, weather and the seasons by using small dabs of colour side by side instead of the traditional blending and glazing techniques. The Impressionists took up the idea and developed it, as did the Pointillist Georges Seurat.

If you try out this technique straight on to a white ground, you may find it difficult to judge the colour balance until you've progressed quite far. One way to avoid this is to work on a toned ground, but another option is to work as our artist did here – scrubbing in the basic colours and tones of each area before applying paint in smaller, thicker doses. She used watercolour paper and small round watercolour brushes, but you can achieve some interesting effects with flat brushes and canvas or board if you prefer.

This broken-colour technique requires practice and a good eye for colour. Our artist has a lot of experience painting in this way, but you may want to keep some scrap paper handy to try out your colour combinations as you go.

◀ **The set-up** The Cornish landscape has long held a fascination for artists because of the beautiful quality of the light. Our artist's love of this area is evident in her painting, but though she has painted the area many times, she doesn't rest on her laurels. She likes to experiment with new colours and varies her style and techniques to give a favourite subject a new lease of life.

◀ **1** Use the No.12 brush to prime the paper with acrylic gesso, working your brushstrokes in one direction to keep the primer as discreet as possible. Leave it to dry.

Plot the positions of the main elements in the scene with the No.3 brush and a thin mix of turps, raw sienna and white. Don't worry about mistakes. Once you are happy with the position of everything, add a little French ultramarine to the mix and emphasize the correct contours. Even now you are free to shift things if you wish, as our artist did during the course of the painting.

YOU WILL NEED

- An 18 x 12in sheet of 140lb fine NOT watercolour paper
- Liquitex acrylic gesso
- Turpentine
- Kitchen towel
- Small mirror (optional)
- Palette
- Painting knife
- Four brushes: a No.12 round hog and three round synthetic watercolour brushes, Nos. 3, 4 and 5
- Twelve oil colours: raw sienna, lemon yellow, Indian yellow, cobalt blue, Winsor blue, French ultramarine, sap green, olive green, scarlet lake, alizarin crimson, permanent magenta and white

Tip

Speed way
To help check her colour mixes, our artist scoops paint up with a painting knife and

holds it up to the subject — giving a more direct comparison than looking from subject to palette. She then holds the knife close to her painting to provide her brush with a handy supply of paint.

◄2 Scrub in the sky with a thin mix of Winsor blue, white and cobalt blue (don't worry about the direction of your brushstrokes). Our artist also dabbed some on to the stone stile with the No.4 brush to indicate its bluish tone. Start to distinguish the bushes and trees with a sap green/Indian yellow mix.

▲3 Use an orange mix of Indian yellow and scarlet lake and a green mix of lemon yellow, cobalt blue, white and Indian yellow for the plants growing over the stones on the left. Apply these with the No.5 round except where you want finer lines, in which case switch to a smaller brush. Now use the green mix to block in the grassy field.

◄4 Mix up some sap green, olive green and magenta to make a dull green for the trees in the background. Use the same mix in the foreground to pick out some of the darker tones.

Stand back to see how the painting is building up so far. The idea is simply to block in the basic tones at this stage. Our artist decided that the tones of the stone in the foreground needed work next (see step 5).

Notice that at this stage the paint has gone on quite thinly. Brushmarks and runs don't matter because you'll be covering this underpainting with thicker paint later.

5 Our artist saw the pink tinge in the white stone, so she scrubbed on some thin magenta to warm the white which would be laid on top. Then she used a mix of cobalt blue, magenta and raw sienna for the dark shadows of the stone and a mix of Winsor blue and magenta where the shadow had a purple tinge.

At this point all the basic blocks of colour should be in, so you can get a good idea of the tonal balance of the composition.

6 Now start to put in the flecks of colour with the No.3 brush, starting with the foreground and using small, directional strokes to show movement. Work fast, putting in each colour as you see it, but keep standing back to get an overview and to check that the optical mixing works. If you spend too long on one area the painting can easily take on a lop-sided look.

7 The house provides a calm interlude in the painting, so give yourself a break from the vigorous foreground work to deal with this and with the position of the fence posts receding into the distance. Don't just rely on the positions which you first put in; check that everything is in its proper place as you paint it.

8 Change to the No.4 brush and continue adding detail to all areas, changing colours constantly and wiping the brush between each change with a kitchen towel so you don't muddy the mixes.

This is an opportunity to experiment and play with the colours. It's possible to make changes all the time, so don't be paralysed with fear – be bold and experiment.

◄9 At this point our artist stood back for another overview. The painting is quickly coming together – the contours of the stones are beginning to appear and the house is sitting well in the landscape. Notice that the stronger colours in the foreground, and the greater contrast between tones, help to bring this area forward.

This is a good point at which to view your painting afresh by looking at its reflection in a mirror.

▲10 Now work on the trees and house. Use a dark blue-green for the fir trees and a soft green mix of Winsor blue, white, lemon yellow and raw sienna for the pine tree to the right of the house. Notice that our artist uses more closely related strips of colour in the background. This helps the area to recede.

Add the windows with a dark grey mix of olive green, ultramarine and white, using your little finger braced against the picture to steady your hand.

◄11 Put more work into the middleground and foreground areas, paying particular attention to the stone. Notice how our artist has indicated each plane on the rock face as well as the changes in colour due to the sunlight and lichen. Look carefully at the set-up photograph and you should be able to make out these variations in colour too.

Now that the main colours have gone in, you can put in some of the grasses in the foreground, as our artist is doing here with a mix of white and Indian yellow. Use mixes based on Indian yellow and scarlet lake for the reddish grasses. These show the wind direction and help to bring the painting to life.

12 Return to the area in front of the stone stile and start to tighten up the details of the plants. Use mixes of French ultramarine, Winsor blue and raw sienna with the addition of olive green in some areas. Put in more grasses at the bottom of the stone stile and pick out some of the individual leaves and flowers in the foreground. Our artist also put a few warm red flecks in the foreground which really help this area to advance.

13 Here you can see how the artist has enlivened the field in the middleground and the stone in the foreground. Notice that the colours in the field are closer in tone than those on the stones in the foreground in accordance with the rules of aerial perspective. However, the artist has used a few of the same greens and pinks in both areas to link them and to lead the viewer deeper into the picture.

14 Add more grasses with a mix of magenta, white, French ultramarine and lemon. Now touch up the stones on the right in the foreground. Add flecks of the green mixes to suggest grasses growing between the slabs. Work on the warmer orange and red tones of the lichen too, and the contrasting purples of the rock.

Now use a dark mix of olive green, Winsor blue and magenta for the deepest shadows under the slabs. Leave this area to dry before working on it again, otherwise the dark colour will sully your next paint layer.

Colour is affected by adjacent colour, so every dab of paint you put down modifies and is modified by the colours which are already there. For this reason it doesn't make sense to finalize just one area of the painting. It is much better to keep the whole thing going, as our artist did in this painting, putting down colour, assessing its impact and adding more colour in response to that until you build up a realistic representation of your subject.

▲ **15** When you are happy with the painting, put in the barbed-wire on the fence with the No.3 brush, dragging just a little paint across the paper and catching some paint from the grasses as you go. These are the first complete horizontal strokes the artist made in the painting.

See how the broken colour captures the light, life and movement of the scene. In the details of the background and foreground (above left) you can see the brushstrokes which combine for a realistic presentation of each area.

Notice, too, how the artist uses the same colours throughout the painting to lead the eye. The same pinks, in particular, are used on the stones on the right, the nearest fence post and the house to draw us deeper into the painting. The same pinks also flicker in the grassy field and on the trees on the right.

Painting with a knife: pineapple

Painting with a knife allows you to cover the support quickly with a wide variety of marks. It also forces you to work boldly and with conviction.

Painting knives are used to apply or scrape away paint from the support. They have very springy, responsive blades made from tempered steel or plastic and the handle is cranked to give some clearance between the artist's hand and the painting. Don't confuse painting knives with palette knives, which are used for mixing paint on the palette and don't have cranked handles.

You can apply the paint in broad sweeps with the flat of the knife, or use the tip to get sharp, angular marks. The edge of the blade makes fine linear marks and you can lift the knife to leave a sticky-looking, spiky texture. You can even skim paint off with the edge of the blade to leave a very thin stain. It isn't difficult to see why knife paintings have richly textured surfaces.

There are two cases where you might want to use a painting knife. The first is where the whole subject calls for the kind of angular marks

and clean edges that a knife can make – such as the pineapple and backdrop in this demonstration. At other times you might use knifework simply to add to your repertoire – alongside brushwork or marks made with your fingers, for example. In any case, knife painting is great fun.

◀ The set-up Choose the right kind of subject. A pineapple is ideal. The fruit has a richly textured surface, with a skin constructed from interlocking geometrical shapes, and the straight edges of its spiky leaves scream out for treatment using the edge of the knife.

▼ 1 Ideally work on an easel. Put it about 2.5-3m from the subject and position it to one side – so you can look from the subject to the canvas. Sketch in the pineapple and the creases on the cloth with charcoal.

Notice how the artist has drawn the fruit off-centre and tilted it, giving it an asymmetrical composition. The folds in the right hand side of the cloth help to balance the drawing.

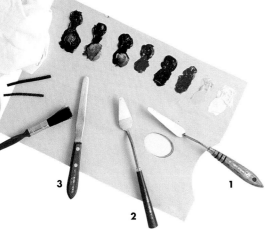

3   1

2

▲ The 90mm long pear-shaped painting knife (1) and the 55mm one (2) are used for applying paint and scraping off. The palette knife (3) is used for mixing paint. Take care of your painting knives, cleaning them after use. Never use them for anything other than painting since the blades are easily damaged.

YOU WILL NEED

- A 50 x 40cm ready primed canvas board
- Charcoal stick
- Clean dry white cotton rags
- Spirits of turpentine
- Two painting knives: a small pear shape about 55mm long; a narrow pear shape about 90mm long
- Palette knife
- Eight oil colours: cadmium yellow, cadmium red, burnt umber, viridian, ultramarine blue, sap green, alizarin crimson, titanium white

◄ 2 Rub in the main colours with a rag and turpsy paint. Cadmium yellow gives the top of the pineapple and cadmium yellow mixed with cadmium red the bottom. Overlay a warm brown – mixed from umber, white and red – to give the middle tone on the right and bottom. Scrub on viridian for leaves.

▼ 3 With the rag, work over the whole surface using ultramarine for the background. Going right up to the edges helps you to assess the tones of the pineapple against the true colour rather than the white of the canvas. Ultramarine mixed with alizarin crimson helps to break up the background.

You can see the artist has painted quickly without fussing. The vigorous green marks already give a sense of growth.

◄ 4 Keeping the painting on the move, use the longer knife to lay on some thicker ultramarine blue. The idea is to start to bring some depth to the painting.

Pick up a good dollop of blue on the underside of the knife and spread it on to the surface as if you were generously buttering bread. Work a few flashes of blue into the leaves too. Clean off the knife on a rag and skim some sap green mixed with cadmium yellow on to the body of the pineapple.

▶ **5** Now work some reds and oranges into the fruit. Don't worry about getting the exact colours at this stage, just introduce some warmer tones.

Mix some alizarin crimson and cadmium yellow and knock back the green you have just put on to the body of the fruit. Introduce some dark pink – as the artist is doing here – by mixing alizarin crimson with white on the canvas itself. Indicate the pattern on the pineapple's surface by applying a stripe or two of crimson with the tip of the knife.

▼ **6** So far you've applied paint mainly in slabs using the flat of the knife but now you can do a bit of drawing with it.

Emphasize the line of the geometrical patterns using the tip of the knife to scratch out the paint. These lines might be obliterated later but in the meantime they serve as a useful reminder. Try to make them go right around the fruit so that they describe the form.

Here the artist has a little cadmium red on the knife while scraping away so that the knife is actually depositing paint at the same time.

▶ **7** Mix up some crimson, cadmium yellow and white to make a slightly tamer orange. Using the flexible tip of the knife, put in the facets of the pineapple between the lines. Hold the knife loosely so that there is a bit of freedom of movement and imagine you are trying to construct a pineapple with your knife. Daub the paint on in thick globules to build up a rich texture.

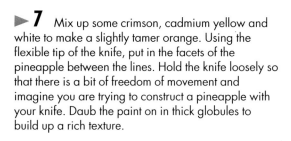

◄ **8** Keep the whole of the painting on the go, never 'finishing' one area before moving on to the next. Return to the background and pick out some of the lighter areas in the cloth.

Lighten some ultramarine with white and, using the flat of the knife, spread the paint thickly. You can see here how broad sweeps give bold, swirling effects.

► **9** Keep stepping back from the easel to get an overview. This helps you decide what to do next.

Here there are some subtle greens, orange-browns, light greens (that are almost lime greens) and an occasional touch of red. In isolation these colours might look odd but seen from a distance they work towards the colour of the pineapple. The leaves need some attention now as does the yellow on the fruit, and the background still looks thin.

▲ **10** Look at the set up on the first page of the demonstration and you'll see that the leaves are not, as you might imagine, a lush green but rather a dusty, greyish-green that tends towards blue rather than yellow. Use white to lighten some viridian and, with the edge of the knife, put on some thick, spiky lines of paint. The technique is rather like printing with the edge of the knife but you can move it about to broaden the lines and get the width of the leaves.

◄ 11 Still using the edge of the knife, put in the leaves on the other side. (Notice here how the artist holds the knife the other way up for comfort and convenience.)

Some of the greens have a little ultramarine blue mixed in. This helps to add depth and leads the eye in. Some thicker cadmium yellow has been laid on to the top left hand side of the fruit – where the light strikes it. This was done using the smaller knife.

▼ 12 The pineapple is the focal point but the background is equally important. So pay it equal attention. The fabric is blue but the light falling on to the folds modulates the tones and even introduces other colours. Observe these carefully.

Using the back of the long knife, elaborate on the light areas using different strength mixes of ultramarine blue and white.

▲ 13 For warm shadows use alizarin crimson mixed with blue and for cooler ones, burnt umber mixed with blue. (You can see q warm violet sandwiched between two strips of light blue just to the right of the pineapple. The cool shadows look almost black. Ultramarine blue mixed with a little cadmium yellow gives the dark green shadow above this.)

Now step back to see how the painting is going and make any final adjustments.

► **14** Here you can see the beautiful qualities that you get in a knife painting. Close to, the paint appears to be in a state of flux with splashes, swirls and blobs of thick paint. These so-called 'happy accidents' often help to capture the spirit of a subject. So before you cover them or scrape them away, consider carefully for a moment whether they add to or detract from the effect. Here they give the sort of burst of energy that is needed to convey growth.

Tip

As a scraper
A knife is excellent for laying on broad, flat areas of thick paint, but remember you can use it to remove paint too – something you can't do as effectively with a brush. You can draw with the knife by scraping the surface with the tip, or you can use the edge to scrape away larger areas. Particularly on canvas, this leaves a stained area that is pleasing to work over.

► **15** In the finished painting, a mix of ultramarine and burnt umber strengthens the shadows around the base of the fruit. Don't labour your painting – taking it too far – or else you'll lose the beautiful immediacy you get with a knife. Leave to dry.

Impasto: texture painting

There's a whole host of strong, eye-catching textures to discover when you come to use the rich, creamy consistency of oil paints straight from the tube.

Impasto is simply oil paint applied to the canvas in thick layers with either a painting knife or brush. The paint needs to be of a buttery consistency – with very little, or even no, turpentine added at all. This means you can make the most of the rich, textural qualities of oils to build up luxuriant layers of impastoed paint. Some artists even add a specially made thickening medium (such as Oleopasto) which improves the body of the paint without increasing the drying time.

In impasto painting, the emphasis is on surface texture. The thick paint actually protrudes from the surface of the support,

breaking the two-dimensional quality of your painting and adding a great sense of energy.

On top of this, you can tease the paint into a variety of shapes and textures – luscious bands of creamy paint; long, thick strokes; ridges; dots and irregular lines of varying widths. In fact, a whole wealth of textural effects opens up which can revolutionize the way you paint.

Because the thick paint retains the strokes you make with knife and brush, the marks you produce are an expressive element in your work. Many artists enjoy this communicative quality, and the odd impulsive brush stroke often adds a charming touch of spontaneity to your painting.

▲ In this painting, the impasto technique is taken to its extreme, with lovely thick applications of buttery paint teased into peaks and ridges.

The work has a rich, painterly feel to it – obviously the artist has really enjoyed the texture of the oils. His dramatic painting is, in fact, just as much about the paint itself as the subject.

'St. Margaret's Bay, Empty Sea' by Arthur Neal, oil on canvas, 14 x 18in

Blades and brushes

Impasto is most often used *alla prima*, i.e. the painting is completed in a single session. You can also use it as the final thick layer when painting fat over lean. Some pictures are painted entirely in impasto, while others use it only in certain areas.

Generally, impasto is painted from dark to light or light over dark.

Painting knives (with cranked handles, unlike palette knives which are straight) make broad marks, while brushes are good for small areas. But whichever you use, remember that changing the angle at which you hold the implement, and using different parts of it, give you different results. Experiment with both to make yourself familiar with the many textures you can achieve.

Knives come in different sizes and shapes that make a variety of marks according to the size of the blade. As with brush marks, a small movement with your wrist results in a fine mark. A large movement with your whole arm gives a larger, more gestural stroke.

Most painting knives are made of metal, but you may prefer a plastic one which is somewhat more flexible. Knives are ideal for blocking in large areas of colour very quickly. And of course, the combination of brush and knife gives you a huge range of marks.

Working with a knife....

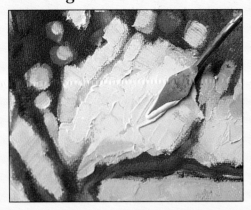

Mix up some thick paint on the palette with your knife, adding a medium such as Oleopasto to give the paint extra body if necessary. Scoop up a generous amount and spread it on the canvas. Work it into broad, textured ridges.

....and a brush

Mix up some thick paint on the palette with a palette or painting knife, adding just enough turpentine to make it workable. Load the brush with paint and apply it thickly to the canvas in short heavy strokes, leaving brush marks.

YOU WILL NEED

- Piece of Fredericks tear off canvas, 18 x 24in (or oil paper with a rough or medium tooth)
- A stick of charcoal
- Seven brushes: No. 11 and 12 chisels; No.4 round bristle; No.4 flat soft; No.50 flat bristle; No.12 bright; No.0 round
- Three pear-shaped painting knives: 55mm, 40mm & 27mm long
- Ultramarine deep alkyd paint
- Eight oil colours: red oxide, cerulean blue, zinc white, alizarin crimson, Naples yellow, Indian yellow, yellow ochre pale, cadmium scarlet

African landscape

▶ **The set-up** The artist worked from this sketch of trees and grassland, made when she lived in Africa. The simple subject is ideal for working on a painting from start to finish in one day.

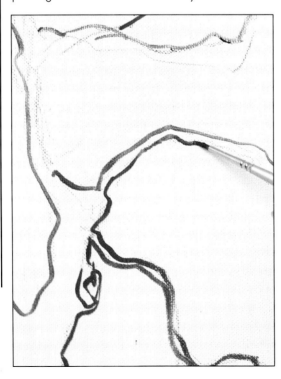

◀ **1** Tape the piece of canvas to your drawing board, and begin by roughly sketching in the general outlines of the trees and their shadows with a stick of charcoal. Dilute some ultramarine deep alkyd paint with plenty of turps so it flows easily and, with the No.0 round brush, paint the outlines of the trees, using the charcoal marks to guide you.

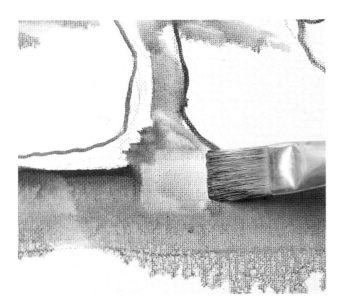

◄ 2 Now roughly paint in the shadows on and under the trees with more dilute ultramarine deep and the No.11 chisel brush. The light is coming from the top left, so the shadows will fall to the right of the trees. Wait for the paint to dry before continuing.

► 3 Dilute some red oxide with plenty of turps to make a thin wash for the underpainting. This warm brick colour will glow through the layers of paint, adding warmth and depth to the final image.

With your No.50 flat brush, begin to lay this wash over the whole of the canvas using broad, horizontal strokes. Don't worry about losing the lines you've already painted – they will still be clear enough for you to work from.

Try to make the paint thinner in some areas and thicker in others to give yourself a lively surface to build on later.

◄ 4 Continue with horizontal strokes for the ground and sky areas, but use shorter vertical dabs of the brush for the areas which will be foliage. Wait for the paint to dry.

Tip

Last is best
Your impasto layer should be the last layer of paint – fat over lean. You can glaze over it with a fine film of paint mixed with glazing medium, but you must not use a thin wash of turpsy paint – it will all crack and fall off.

► 5 Use a less diluted version of the same colour to strengthen the bark of the foreground tree. Don't lay the colour on flat, but try to show the darker tones with the less dilute paint. Being in the foreground, and almost dead in the centre of the canvas, this tree is an important part of the composition. Use ultramarine blue again to build up the darker shadows on the trees with the No.4 flat soft brush.

6 Brush in the shape of the foliage with the No.11 chisel, using dilute red oxide with a touch of ultramarine deep. Use lively vertical strokes to contrast with the horizontal ones of the underpainting.

Do the same for the other trees, strengthening the bark and dabbing in the foliage. The trunks and branches make a skeleton on which you can build the shape of the whole tree. Vary the spaces between the branches, especially in the trees that recede into the background.

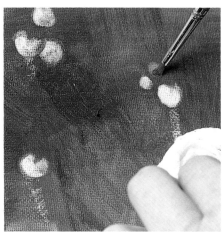

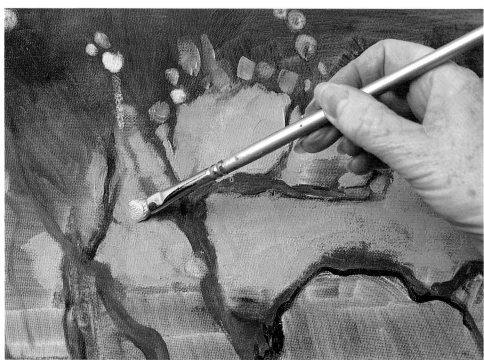

7 Take out small circles of paint on the trees with the No.4 round bristle brush dipped in turps. Use kitchen towel to stop the turps dribbling down the canvas – this will ruin the shapes of the circles. (At a later stage, you will fill these circles with bright, orange paint to depict the fruit).

8 Now for the sky. Make a mix of cerulean blue and zinc white, diluted 50:50 with turps, and paint the sky all the way to the horizon line with the No.4 flat brush. This blue is the complementary of the deep russet orange used in the underpainting. The 'play' between the two gives sparkle to the whole painting.

Sharpen up the shape of the trees by picking out the background, working on the negative shapes between the tree branches. Try to contrast large and small areas.

9 When you have covered the sky, allow the paint to dry a little before moving on to the next stage. It doesn't have to dry completely – the surface needs to be tacky to the touch to be workable. Take advantage of these waiting periods to stand back from your painting and see exactly what needs to be done next.

While you're waiting for the sky to dry, extend the shadows under the trees using ultramarine blue, with the No.12 bright.

◄ **10** Now for some impasto. Mix cerulean blue, zinc white and a touch of alizarin crimson on the palette with the 27mm long painting knife. Don't mix in any turps – use pure paint. Scoop up some paint and spread it over the surface of the sky with the back of the knife. The paint should remain quite thick, so don't spread it out too thinly.

Tip

Extra texture
You can give the paint even more texture by scratching into the surface with anything you choose. You can even make imprints! Sand and sawdust can be added to oils to create rich, highly textured areas within paintings.

◄ **11** When the paint has dried a little, use the No.4 soft flat brush and more of the same colour to re-define the gnarled, knobbly branches, and the negative spaces of sky in between. Use the 40mm long knife to blend the paint on the surface of the painting, adjusting the colours of the sky.

► **12** Blend a mixture of Indian yellow, Naples yellow, and yellow ochre pale on your palette and leave it to become tacky. When it's ready, pick it up with the No.50 large flat bristle brush and make short, vertical dabs with the brush here and there to indicate the clumps of dry grass in the foreground.

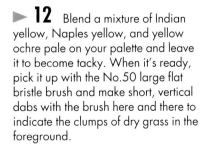

▶ **13** With the same mixture, use the smaller No.12 chisel brush to make horizontal strokes and vertical dabs to blend the paint into the background using a wet-in-wet technique. The smaller brush makes smaller marks which help to give a sense of distance towards the background.

◀ **14** With the 55mm long painting knife, apply a mixture of Naples yellow and zinc white between the shadows and around the base of the first tree to bring out the shapes and add contrast. Build up the surface to give a rich painterly feel.

▼ **15** Continue using the same mix to lighten the areas between the shadows under each of the trees.

▶ **16** With the edge of the 40mm painting knife, scrape back some of the Naples yellow and zinc white mix you used under the trees in the previous step. This varies the texture of the grass. Now use a mixture of cerulean blue and zinc white to put in some cool shadows under the trees with the 55mm painting knife. To establish the ground plane, use sweeping horizontal strokes. This is a good example of using the texture of impasto to give form.

▶ **17** Mix some Indian yellow and cadmium scarlet to make a vibrant orange for the fruit. Touch this into the blank circles on the trees where you lifted out the paint earlier. Use the No.4 round bristle brush for this. Add small areas of white for highlights (inset).

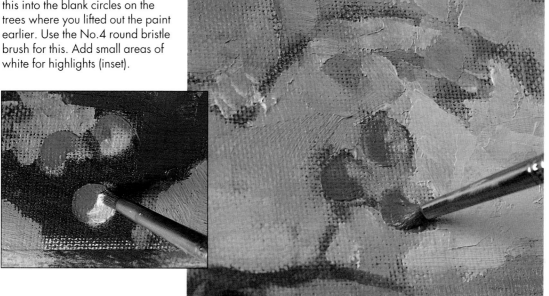

Tip

A new view
When you are working on a painting continuously it's sometimes hard to see the wood for the trees! Give yourself a fresh view of your work by leaving the room and coming back to look at it half an hour or so later.

► **18** Put in the horizon line with pure zinc white. Use your No.4 flat to make short, vertical dabs of the brush. With the same brush add a few finishing touches to the sky in between the trees where it needs more definition. Where necessary, crisp up the edges of the branches with the sky mix and add some more impasto if the picture surface looks too flat.

▼ **19** If you find that some areas of paint don't mix into the painting well, blend them in with a wide, flat brush. Don't overdo it, though – you'll end up with a smeared mess. Keep your colours clean and fresh so the picture retains a sense of immediacy like the finished painting here. The strength of the colours and the texture of the grassland have really captured the atmosphere of a scorching African landscape.

Achieving bold brushwork

Your brushstrokes contribute a great deal to the impact of your paintings, so it's vital to practise and build up confidence.

Tight, hesitant brushwork often leaves its mark on a painting – it can look stifled and forced. But practice gives you confidence, and the ease to make spontaneous, expressive brushstrokes. This fluency develops over time, but, as with many techniques, you can't go wrong looking at the work of other artists to give you ideas.

In the paintings on this page and the project overleaf, the quick, expressive brushwork adds to the charm of the work. The artist's speed and assurance in applying paint help to capture the moment, and something of the movement within the scene.

Follow the steps of this project and try to echo the fluidity and vigour of the brushwork. There are other valuable lessons to learn, too. Few of the colour mixes are suggested, giving you the chance to create them yourself. Alternatively, change the colour scheme – you might want to put in a different range of colours for the saris, or give the sea a greener tinge. If you do invent your own colour scheme, consider it carefully and try to achieve a good balance of colour and tone.

You'll need a diluent for the glazes – our artist prefers artists' painting medium (Winsor & Newton). There are a variety of thinning agents for oils you could try, or simply stick to turpentine. You'll need linseed oil to give the colours a jewel-like shine in areas. Again, we haven't suggested where or when to use it, so rely on your own discretion. Use it to make the bright colours glow, or to enrich darker hues.

▲ **Brisk yet well-considered brushstrokes capture the energy and vitality of this beach scene. The brushstrokes are really free where they sum up the mass of trees in the background. This way they don't lead the eye away from the foreground figures.**
'Ladies on Kodalam Beach' by Kay Gallwey, oil on canvas, 8 x 10in

◄ **You can almost feel the speed and energy at which this beach scene was painted, especially the areas in the background – the beach umbrellas and undergrowth. These spirited areas of the painting serve as a contrast to the more leisurely depiction of the two women in the foreground, sharing a quiet moment. The contrast helps to emphasize their pensive mood.**
'Sun and Shade' by Kay Gallwey, oil on canvas, 9½ x 13in

Beach walk, Kerala

The set-up On her travels in India, our artist compiled a wealth of reference material. She arrived at this composition using several sketches and photos taken in Kerala, a region on the south-western coast. She simplified the landscape to a mere suggestion so the figures could take centre stage.

◄**1** Tone your ground with pale blue, using a clean cotton rag to give the picture an energetic start. Dip the rag in artist's painting medium, then into your colour and spread it across the canvas. Scrub a clean section of the rag across the surface to even out the tone.

Strengthen the blue mix slightly and, with the small brush, roughly draw the figures, the water's edge and the coastline and hill. Wipe away mistakes with your rag or finger. Emphasize the diagonal surf line with quick, rough strokes of white.

YOU WILL NEED

- ☐ A 12 x 18in stretched linen canvas
- ☐ Turpentine and linseed oil
- ☐ Artists' painting medium
- ☐ Clean cotton rags
- ☐ Mahlstick
- ☐ Palette
- ☐ Three flat hog hair brushes: large, medium and small
- ☐ Fourteen Schminke oil colours: titanium white, cadmium yellow middle, Indian yellow, raw sienna, vermilion red tone, purple rose permanent, flesh colour 4 (deep), indigo, manganese cerulean blue, royal blue light, cobalt violet light opaque, sap green, burnt umber, lamp black
- ☐ One Daler-Rowney oil colour: monestial turquoise

▶**2** Apply a pale yellow glaze for the sand around the figures, and a pale purple one to start off the reflections in the puddle under the figures.

Use purple rose permanent, raw sienna, flesh colour and cadmium yellow middle to make a series of light and dark flesh tones. Apply them in quick brushstrokes to catch the shapes of the faces, arms and midriffs. (Apply paint thinly to allow for subsequent layers.) Paint the hair black, enlivened with blue or red. Use the angle of the women's windswept hair to indicate the wind direction.

Paint the saris using thicker paint. Pick a colour for each one and apply it in light and dark tones to indicate the fabric folds. Use quick strokes of the large flat brush for a loose, sketchy application.

◄**3** Work across the group of women, painting in the saris and still using rapid, sketchy strokes. The large and small brushes allow for a good variety of marks. Although you'll strengthen and modify the colours later, it's sensible to establish the general balance of colour and tone now, and build on this foundation as you continue. Don't use thick paint, so you can overpaint later.

Here, our artist adds dabs of intense, pure colour to the saris to indicate areas she intends to brighten.

▶ **4** With the large flat brush, paint the contours of the distant hill and coastline in single strokes of colour. Indicate tree trunks with vertical dabs of the end of the bristles. Use yellow, greens and indigo, as well as some appropriate colours from the saris.

Combine a pale blue with white for the water. Allow the colours to blend on the canvas as you drag the brush horizontally across the surface. This creates a streaky texture to indicate gentle waves. Re-emphasize the diagonal line of frothy surf with rapid white strokes.

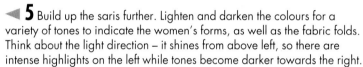

◀ **5** Build up the saris further. Lighten and darken the colours for a variety of tones to indicate the women's forms, as well as the fabric folds. Think about the light direction – it shines from above left, so there are intense highlights on the left while tones become darker towards the right.

Notice how the glaze of the shallows has been applied in different directions to suggest broken reflections. Dab a touch of each sari colour into the area beneath it to heighten the impression of reflections.

▶ **6** Develop the dark and pale flesh tones, always bearing in mind the direction the light is coming from. Blend the tones together to indicate the smooth texture of the skin. Indicate the wetness of the saris by using slightly darker tones below the knees.

At this point, our artist made a couple of important changes. She decided the sari fabric floating over the shoulder of the figure on the far left conflicted with the wind direction, so she painted it out. She also changed the hairstyle of the same figure and used this to show the wind direction instead.

◀ **7** Build up the reflections. With the medium flat brush take colour from the hem of each sari into the reflection beneath (above left). Adding a little green, use diminishing horizontal strokes to show each reflection (left). Apply a green glaze around the foreground for balance.

8 Use the small flat to build up and blend skin tones and sharpen details on the figures. Make careful, considered strokes on fine areas such as these. Our artist used a mahlstick to steady her hand for fine work. If you don't have one, use a length of dowel – rest one end on the side of your easel and lean your hand on it to give more control.

9 Bring out the surf with brisk, bold brushstrokes. Add some intense Indian yellow highlights on the figures, then put in the finishing touches on the saris and the facial details. Use burnt umber, varying the tone with raw sienna to indicate the necks and jaw lines.

10 Our artist felt the shallows didn't look wet enough, so she washed in more of the same colours diluted with plenty of artists' painting medium. Apply these liberally, allowing the paint to drip. These dribbles help to emphasize the wet look.

   The brisk, sketchy brushstrokes are clearly visible in the painting, creating liveliness. They also help the composition by emphasizing the feeling of a moment captured, in a way that hesitant brushstrokes could not. Notice the movement and vitality of the women, and the way the surf looks as though it will recede into the sea at any moment.

Using warm and cool colours

If faced with a dull day, seek out the subtle play of warm and cool colours. You may find you have the basis of a lively painting, full of depth and interest.

The painting shown here is an excellent example of an artist making something out of nothing. The intention was to paint a sunny seaside scene, but on the day allotted the skies were leaden and the chilly wind sent the normal seaside crowds scurrying for cover. Undaunted, our artist set up his easel on the shingle beach at a point where a fishing boat was drawn up above the tide mark.

He worked on a small scale on a board toned with a raw sienna ground. Despite the lack of sunlight, he produced an image full of colour – exploiting colour relationships, particularly the contrasts of warm and cool neutrals, then contrasting these with pure colours.

First he blocked in the main outlines in cerulean blue, which shimmers against the warm ground. He then mixed a cool neutral grey for the sky and a warm neutral for the beach, scumbling on the colour so the ground showed through in places, modifying the overlaid tones to create a complex, broken effect.

Next he touched in the hot red of the boat – notice how this pure colour sizzles against the surrounding neutrals. Notice also that it is placed on a key location, which draws the eye. This spot is reinforced by the sweep of the walkway, the horizon line and the masts, which ensure the eye returns to this small, bright area. Patches of clear, bright blue counterpoint the red, enhancing its warmth and creating a satisfying sense of balance.

Elsewhere you find pearly tones comprised of subtly orchestrated warms and cools – salmon pink against mauves and violets, russets and hyacinth blue, cerulean and terracotta. The colours appear to shimmer above the surface, capturing the ambiguous quality of the wind-swept, moisture-laden skies.

The set-up Our artist chose this view because of the range of warm and cool muted colours. He liked the fishing boat with its bright red stripe against the neutral warm beach tones and the cool neutral grey of the sky.

1 Start the play of warm and cool tones with the ground – tone it with a warm golden brown based on raw sienna. Apply it with vertical strokes of the decorators' brush. Once dry, draw the main outlines in cerulean blue with the small round brush.

Loosely block in the sky with the medium filbert and a pale, cool grey mixed from white with touches of blue black/yellow ochre. Let this blend with some of the blue towards the right, creating a slightly cooler hue.

Paint the pebbly beach with a warm tone. For this, modify the sky mix by adding more yellow ochre then apply it with free strokes. Vary the proportions of the colours in the mix, blending them together on the board to achieve a lively surface. Keep each variation warm, since the subtle contrast between the cool sky and the warmer pebbles creates a pleasing tension in the composition.

YOU WILL NEED

- [ ] An 8 x 10in piece of hardboard covered with stretched linen and primed
- [ ] Turpentine
- [ ] Four brushes: a ½in decorators' brush and three hog hair brushes – a large flat, a medium filbert and a small round
- [ ] Palette and palette knife
- [ ] Easel
- [ ] Twelve oil colours: titanium white, Naples yellow, yellow ochre, vermilion, alizarin crimson, cadmium red, ultramarine, cerulean blue, burnt sienna, raw sienna, burnt umber and blue black

▲ Rather than waste left-over oil paints after finishing a painting, our artist mixes the remnants from his palette and uses this to tone the ground on several supports, ready for future sessions. You can also scrape your paints off the palette into an air-tight container. This should keep them fresh enough to reuse when you come to paint again.

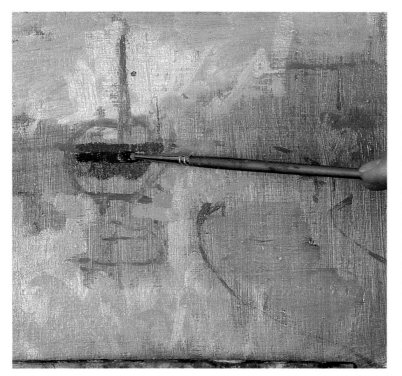

◀ **2** Use a mid blue and the medium filbert to block in areas of the walkway and paint the side of the distant building to the right. Balance this by putting in the brick building in front in a warm pinky brown. Paint the red decorative line on the boat's stern with cadmium red, then use this and the tone of the walkway to help you gauge the tones of the other colours on the boat. Try a dark, steely grey-blue for the hull, and for the keel a deep chocolate brown.

Since the tonal contrasts are so subtle, test your mixes: dab a blob on the painting to check its relationship with other hues.

▶ **3** Use the steely grey-blue to pick out the distant pier. Block in the sea beneath the pier with a warm primrose yellow, overlaying this with a pale grey-blue (notice the shimmering effect created by overlaying a warm colour with a cool one).

Indicate the dinghy by the boat with a dull blue mix and suggest the shadow beneath it with a near-black mix. Use this to paint the boat's mast. Place the post by the dinghy and the lobster pot in grey-brown. Indicate the figures with swift near-black lines.

◀ **4** For the purposes of perspective, you need to fill out the closest figure – the background ones can remain quite small. Our artist chose a shade of red for the jersey, to balance the decorative red line on the boat.

Add the smaller mast on the boat with a mid grey. Use some of the colour from the pebble beach, warmed with Naples yellow for the curve of the low wall to the right of the walkway.

◀**5** Continue working on the right side of the painting, developing the background by picking out general details. Bring on the walkway, defining its curved outline.

Then, to balance this, warm up the pebbly beach, adding a touch of burnt sienna to the original beach mix.

Continue to adjust tones in this way as the painting progresses, creating a pleasing contrast between warm and cool. With a couple of quick brushstrokes, paint in a child, holding an arm up to the figure in the red jersey. All these dashes of colour help give the foreground an air of bustle.

Tip

Handling details

Our artist painted the seated figure loosely, but found he

needed to clarify the outlines a little. He wanted to avoid fine lines so as to keep the style consistent with the rest of the painting. He therefore used the end of a brush handle to draw in the outlines — a type of sgraffito. This allowed him to keep the details quite vague, yet distinguished the figure clearly from the background, pulling it forward in space.

▶**6** Add another figure to the foreground left to balance all the action on the right side of the composition. Use the medium filbert for this to avoid becoming too detailed. Loosely indicate the face, hair and clothes with a combination of warm and cool muted colours.

At this stage the light changed, bringing a touch of warmth to the sky in places. Our artist mixed a pale yellow neutral to stroke into the right side of the sky. Then he lightened the pebbly beach with a similar warm neutral.

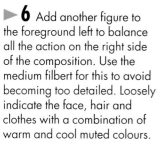

◀**7** Look back at step 6 and run an imaginary diagonal line from the bottom left of the painting to the top right. Our artist did this to check the balance of the composition and found the upper triangle looked heavier than the lower one, because there seemed to be something missing from the left side of the lower area. He filled this gap with a seated figure. Again, don't go into detail when painting in the figure (see Tip above).

▶ **8** For more interest in the foreground, roughly suggest another figure on the walkway. Then add the finishing touches. Tighten the walkway edges a little with a deeper tone, and use a muted grey-lilac to indicate a few shadows and break up the tone of the path.

Add or change as you wish to improve things – our artist dotted in two white lifebuoys on a pole along the path to aid perspective (see below).

▼ **9** All the shifts, adjustments and modifications our artist made through the progress of this painting have paid off in the final image, which plays on the subtle contrast between warm and cool neutrals. Most of the tones are very close, and the balance of warm and cool colours works excellently, capturing the atmosphere of a rainy day at the seafront.

Painting skin tones

The human face offers a wonderful and exciting challenge to the artist. Don't be put off if you've never attempted a portrait before – you'll be surprised how much you can learn from it.

Although you may think you know a lot about the human face, you probably don't notice as much as you think. With close friends, in particular, we tend to look only at the eyes and mouth, rather than the details. Try this by drawing a friend from memory. It's hard, but don't be put off. The key to a portrait is not to attempt to do too much at first. Think of the face as an ordinary, if complex, three-dimensional object. Capturing character can follow later.

For this exercise, concentrate on accurately rendering the colours you see. Remember, there are many variations. At first you'll only be able to distinguish a few basic differences, such as the pink in the cheeks and a greenish tinge in the eye sockets. But as you look, you'll spot subtle differences where the shadows merge into the lights. With practice, you'll also learn what to look for – reflected colours from clothing, and pinkish tones where the bone or cartilage lie close to the surface (on the ears, nose, cheekbone, forehead and chin).

Block in the basic colours first, then refine them as you start to see more tones. Remember, warm colours come forward, while cooler colours recede, so if you have trouble in making the face look three dimensional, you can warm up or cool down a colour to put it in its proper place.

Oils are a good choice for your first portrait because they are so malleable – you can adjust and refine your work as you go along. Try out colours you think will work. If you don't like one, wipe it off with a turpsy rag, or modify it with another colour. Don't be afraid to experiment, because that's the way to discover new colour mixes and combinations. Keep your paint fairly thin at first (remember the principle of fat over lean) and you'll find adjustments are easy.

For the portrait that follows our artist chose to work on canvas tinted with a rough wash of burnt sienna and ultramarine thinned with lots of turps. She always works on a toned ground because it gives a mid tone against which to judge all the lights and darks. If you do the same, you'll need to tint the canvas several days in advance to give it a chance to dry out before you start painting – or use acrylic.

▼ Here the artist chose to include the attractive room setting which conveys something about the sitter's reflective character.

This portrait took several days to complete. Take time over yours too. If you work in short sessions it gives you time to assess your painting afresh.
'Mrs Letitia Brett' by Anne Wright, oil on canvas, 36 x 24in

Portrait of a gentleman

◄ **The set-up** Our artist used a photograph for this painting. Although it's generally better to paint from life, you'll find that a photograph provides good back-up – you can carry on when your sitter gets tired.

▼**1** Using the No.2 bright and a mix of burnt sienna, cobalt blue and turps, sketch in the face and shoulders and shade in the basic dark tones to give dimension. Stand back to assess proportions and make adjustments. You can alter or obliterate any mistakes later.

Our artist established the positions of her sitter's features quite firmly so she could relax later on, but you may prefer more sketchy shapes at this stage. You can find the exact positions as you paint.

▼**2** Start on the face with the mid tones, using your No.3 bright. Use a mix of cadmium red, yellow ochre, white and a touch of olive green for the warmish pink, and a mix of white, cadmium red, yellow ochre and a touch of cobalt blue for the cooler shadows. Modify the mixes as you go to give the face more form.

For the eyebrows and hair, use white, tinted with cobalt and raw umber. See how the hair takes shape when some of the lights and darks are established. For the eyes, our artist used olive green, cobalt and sepia.

◄ **3** Now establish the colours of the background and clothing, scumbling on thin paint diluted with turps. Once the background is in, notice that the colours of the face need modifying – a colour is always affected by others adjacent to it.

Our artist used various mixes of cobalt, viridian and a touch of burnt sienna for the background. For the jumper she mixed burnt sienna, alizarin crimson, cobalt, yellow ochre and white. For the darks in the jumper she used burnt umber, alizarin crimson and ultramarine.

▼ **4** This is a good point to take a break. When you come back to the painting, you can assess what is needed. At this stage you can still adjust the position of the features if you wish.

Refine the lights and darks with your No.1 or No.2 bright, adding white to your paint mixes for solidity, and using less turps with the paint.

▼ **5** Now blend the colours already established. Soften the lines from the nose to the mouth, add some more tones to the hair and develop the eyebrows, neck and ears.

Work on the eyes. These are spheres under the lids, so shade them accordingly with one of your round brushes. Our artist used white tinted with olive green, ultramarine and a little raw umber for the whites. Then she added the pinks at the inner edge of the eye. To add a twinkle to the eyes, touch in a splash of white dulled with yellow ochre near the edge of the iris.

▲ **6** Now attend to the background so it doesn't lag behind the face. Use mixes of viridian, your blues, black and the yellows. (Don't develop it too much, though — it should play second fiddle to the face.)

Develop the shirt with white tinted with cobalt, a little yellow ochre and raw umber. Add a little cadmium red for the reflections of the jumper. Then work on the jumper, using the colours from step 3. To send the background back, darken the area behind the head — our artist used mixes of ultramarine, olive and burnt umber.

◄ **7** Our artist continued to work on the face, developing each area bit by bit. Compare this step with step 2. See how far the face has developed, then trace back through the steps to see how this was achieved. Look at the areas of light, and compare the warm and cool tones.

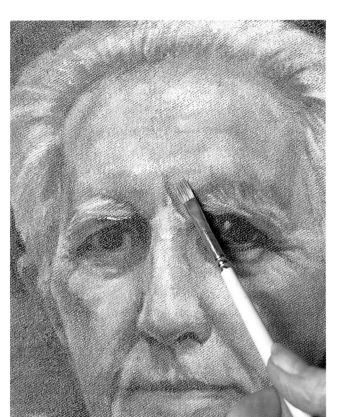

◄8 Our artist left the picture for a while so she could reassess the colours once they were dry. When she came back to it, she scumbled paint over the face to knock back the colour a little, then reworked the lines on the forehead and around the eyes.

If you've allowed the paint to dry on your portrait, it's a good idea to do what our artist did and apply a thin layer of paint over the top. This provides a workable surface for blending in new layers of colour. If you don't want to alter the existing colour, use a thin layer of oil, such as linseed oil, instead.

SOLVE IT

Send back the background

If you study your sitter carefully, you should be able to see that the background forms a slightly darker outline around him or her. You can add this outline either by painting the background over the edge of the figure, as our artist did on the shoulders, or simply by darkening the background around the figure. See how this brings the figure forward.

◄▲9 Now our artist went to work on the background again. Notice how it 'blues' as it recedes – creating a sense of depth (inset, above). Even if you see the background as solid blocks of colour, vary the tones slightly to create more interest. Keep the background fairly loose or blurred – this helps to focus attention on the figure.

◄10 Check your figure looks fully three-dimensional. If it doesn't, bring the front areas forward with warmer, brighter mixes, and send the cheeks back with cooler, darker mixes. In general, the face is pinker where the bone or cartilage is near the surface – on cheeks, chin, forehead, nose and ears. The colours become more yellowish or even greenish under the nose and on the fatty area between nose and cheek. Also make sure your light direction is consistent.

▼11 Compare the finished portrait with the original photograph (inset). Can you make out all the colour differences on the face that our artist has seen and put in?

Notice that our artist changed the sitter's jacket into a red jumper. The red works well because it's the complementary colour of the green background, and being warm, it automatically advances. She also changed the blue reflections on the white shirt to red accordingly.

Making use of a mid tone

Artists have painted on a toned ground for centuries – and for good reason. There are distinct advantages in starting with a canvas that already has some colour on it.

A carefully chosen toned ground can provide a good mid tone, against which you can judge your lights and darks. This means that the tonal relationships can be established quickly. It's also easier to judge them accurately.

A toned ground acts as a link between disparate areas of colour, so that, even at an early stage, the picture reads as a whole. You can see this linking effect in the painting below. If the overlying paint layers are loosely applied, it may show through the final painting to provide one of the main colours, as in the picture on the right, or it may contribute to a complex broken-colour effect.

However, you should note that toning the ground will affect the colour of overlying paint layers. Some artists feel that for a brilliant, sparkling effect you need to work on a white ground.

One final point is worth making. Although there's something very enticing about a pure white surface, it can be very daunting – presenting an awful vista of the work needing to be done. A toned ground makes this whole prospect much easier – you don't have to screw up courage to put down the first mark on a coloured canvas!

▼ The toned ground shows through in large areas, providing the mid tone and creating a lively working feel.
'Sarah' by Brenda Holtam, oil on board, 9 ½ x 7in

▼ Here, the toned ground is left to show through in only a few areas of the painting. However, it has an important role to play, modifying the colours on top, and unifying the different elements.
'St. Mary's, Battersea' by Dennis Gilbert, oil on canvas, 18 x 14in

Vases of anemones

▶ **The set-up** Take care when arranging your flowers. Find the main focal point and consider whether a landscape, portrait or square format is most suitable. Look too for the main direction of light – it affects tonal values and shadows.

This painting uses 15 colours, so lay them out methodically on your palette – warm colours on one side, cool colours on another. Our artist used a handful of small brushes, all of a similar size; he restricted each brush to one colour. This isn't absolutely necessary, but it does mean you don't have to keep cleaning the brushes.

YOU WILL NEED

- ☐ A stretched canvas or canvas board 25 x 35cm, toned with a thin wash of raw sienna and raw umber diluted with turpentine

- ☐ A series of small bristle bright brushes for the flowers and a small bristle chisel brush for the background

- ☐ Easel; palette; palette knife

- ☐ 2B pencil; sketch pad

- ☐ Turps; linseed oil

- ☐ Thirteen oil colours: cadmium scarlet, alizarin crimson, purple madder alizarin, permanent mauve, cerulean blue, cobalt blue deep, ultramarine, terre verte, cadmium green, raw sienna, yellow ochre, burnt sienna, flake white

▼ **2** Using a small sable brush, make a dilute mix of terre verte with turps. Divide the edges of your ready toned canvas into four and square it up, just as you did with the sketch. Mix some cobalt blue deep with the terre verte to strengthen it, and mark the position of the flowers on the canvas.

▶ **3** Put in a few touches of local colour, blocking in the main elements with cadmium scarlet, cadmium green mixed with a touch of yellow ochre for the foliage, permanent mauve, purple madder alizarin and white. Feel your way into the picture, trying to convey the general overall idea. Notice how the cup and vase have been redrawn.

▼ **1** Make a quick sketch of the flowers using the soft pencil. Draw a rectangle of the same proportion as the canvas you intend to use for the still life. Divide each side into four equal divisions, dividing one side in half then the two divisions in half again. This is called 'squaring up' and is useful for transferring and enlarging pictures from one surface to another.

▲ **4** Start building up touches of colour, readjusting shapes and proportions. Use permanent mauve, alizarin crimson and ultramarine for the mug, with white for a lighter tone. Work evenly across the surface, using spots of recessive colour for reference points, so you can plan the position of the flowers.

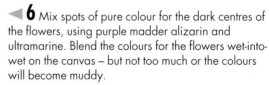

▲ **5** Take the small chisel brush and, using horizontal and vertical brushstrokes, block in some of the background colour. Mix a variety of blues using cobalt blue, ultramarine, tiny smudges of yellow ochre and flake white.

◄ **6** Mix spots of pure colour for the dark centres of the flowers, using purple madder alizarin and ultramarine. Blend the colours for the flowers wet-into-wet on the canvas – but not too much or the colours will become muddy.

► **7** Mix white and yellow ochre to make a warm white for the white anemone in the foreground. Mix a cold white using white, cobalt blue, yellow ochre and a touch of cadmium scarlet for the white anemone behind it. The warmer white advances and makes this anemone appear in front of the cooler one.

▶ **8** The picture is building up slowly. Don't be tempted to bother with detail; concentrate on shape and colour. Look at negative shapes too. In places the shape of a flower can be formed by painting in the background – such as the leaves underneath the purple anemone.

▼ **9** Use warm and cool colours to make some flowers (or parts of a flower) come forward or go backwards. Paint in the red anemone, using warm cadmium scarlet for the outer rim of the petals and a cooler alizarin crimson for the inner part of the flower.

▶ **10** Keep the edge of the table loosely defined, so that attention is focused on the main flowers. Make sure the table top becomes slightly lighter in tone as it comes towards you. For the table, mix a range of interesting neutrals using white, with touches of raw sienna or burnt sienna cooled with ultramarine. Add minute amounts of other colours to warm them up or cool them down.

Tip

Keep things clean

It's easy to get the white paint on your palette dirty, especially if you keep going back to it with a dirty brush. Our artist used three squeezes of white paint on his palette, then picked up small amounts with a palette knife to mix with other colours. This kept his whites clean.

◄**11** Mix pure ultramarine and purple madder alizarin for the cup, lightening it with white at one edge and leaving the coloured ground to act as the other highlighted edge. Don't leave any hard edges – soften them with a fairly dry brush.

▼**12** Now you should be led more by the painting than by the still life in front of you. The picture starts to take over. Does it need changing or defining in some places? Here our artist has added a leaf to break the background edge which coincides with the edge of a red flower.

▼**13** Now mix two-thirds turpentine to one-third linseed oil. Use this glaze to add the final details over the wet paint. It helps to prevent the paint from spreading. Add highlights on to the lighter tones of green, using white, yellow ochre and raw sienna.

14 Notice how the blue shadow helps to define the white anemone lying on its side. Use the same blue mix you made for the background. This serves to unify the picture. Paint in the stems using a mix of cadmium yellow, white and your blues.

The small touches of highlights on the stem, with the shadows underneath, make it look as though you could pick the flowers off the painting! Notice, too, how your mid-toned surface still shows through in places, supporting the strong, bright colours of the flowers.

SOLVE IT

Scraping back

After step 10 our artist felt the blue background had become too dark and too thick to paint over (something that easily happens if you are painting alla prima or wet-into-wet). He used a palette knife to scrape off some of the background paint, then applied a lighter mix of blue over the whole area.

15 There are very few hard edges in this painting. The focal point is concentrated at the front, so keep the rest soft and out of focus. Look how the larger red anemone is brought forward by making the background darker.

Throughout the painting, our artist was constantly adjusting his colours by adding small touches of others. Often he defined the edge of a flower by painting in the background (back to negative and positive shapes again).

A country kitchen

In this project, our artist shows just what you can achieve in a corner of your home and how to use the ready-toned ground of MDF board to get you off to a flying start !

To get the best from this project, set up a still life of your own. Following basics such as working fat over lean and from a toned ground, consolidate some of the things you've learnt so far. Try any techniques you think might work well for your subject – scumbling or impasto, for example – but don't go overboard. (Our artist used his solid command of tone and colour rather than relying on any particular technique.)

Try working on medium density fibre (MDF) board. It's inexpensive and self-supporting and comes in a range of delightfully warm colours – which means the ground is already toned for you. Buy a piece larger than you require (you can saw it to size when your painting has dried). Sand it to give it a slight tooth, and rub the surface with a rag soaked in a 50/50 mix of turps and linseed oil. This helps prevent the board from sucking the oil from the paint too quickly. You'll find that the paint dries to an attractive matt finish.

▲ **The set-up** The grey-greens of the chest and the greys on the wall give this subject a subtle look. But contrast between the buffs of the onions and board, and the blue of the stripes provides ample colour excitement. Subdued lighting from behind the curtain raises highlights on the board, onions and leeks, but there are plenty of rich shadows here too.

◀ **1** Sketch a few guidelines with a mix of white and Payne's gray and a No.6 filbert brush. Then block in the main forms, aiming roughly for the colours you see in your subject. Mix viridian, Payne's gray and white for the chest (a touch of cobalt blue and/or cadmium yellow might help).

▶ **2** Block in the background with a No.8 round brush, using lighter and darker mixes of white and Payne's gray. As the wall recedes add cobalt blue. Leave the potatoes for the moment. Instead, mix some burnt umber, yellow ochre and Payne's gray and, with a No.4 round brush, tick in the items resting on the chest.

YOU WILL NEED

- ☐ A 76 x 50cm piece of MDF board
- ☐ Sandpaper
- ☐ Six brushes: No.6 filbert, No.8 round, No.4 round, No.4 filbert, No.6 long flat, No.2 flat
- ☐ Fourteen colours: viridian, Payne's gray, titanium white, cobalt blue, cadmium yellow, ultramarine, burnt umber, yellow ochre, cadmium lemon, raw sienna, burnt sienna, alizarin crimson, ivory black cadmium red
- ☐ Pure linseed oil
- ☐ Pure spirits of turpentine; white spirit
- ☐ Cotton rag; 2 dippers

◄ 3 Here our artist uses his fingertips to blend some white into the leeks. The idea is to make a smudgy indication of colour, position and tone.

Mix white, cadmium lemon, a touch of cobalt blue and yellow ochre to make a pale yellowy green. With your No.4 filbert brush, touch in the leeks and then blend some white into the ends with your fingertips.

► 4 Using the same brush and mix you used for the leeks, paint the asparagus stalks. For the tops, which are darker, add a little ultramarine.

For the onions, mix cadmium red, yellow ochre, cadmium yellow and white and paint them in with a No.4 round brush. Paint the shadows under the onions with a mix of burnt umber, yellow ochre and white.

► 5 Paint the board using the No.6 long flat brush and a mix of yellow ochre, white and raw sienna. (For the side of the board, add Payne's gray.) Assess the tones on top of the chest. If they need to be darker, add more Payne's gray to the viridian mix from step 1.

Paint the bowl's stripes with a No.4 filbert brush and a mix of cobalt blue, Payne's gray and a touch of black. Work the white/Payne's gray mix you used for the wall in between the stripes with a No.2 flat brush. Use the same mix with a No.8 round for the potato bowl and its shadow.

Tip

Intermixing

Often, you'll find that you can get just the effect you're after by merging together the colour on your brush with wet paint already on the support. Here the brown that's on the brush mixes accidentally with the blue of the stripe to make a dark shadow under the bowl.

▲ **6** Use the greys from step 2 to re-model the bowls where necessary. For the shadows on the onions use a darker mix of the one in step 4. Touch in the knobs with some Payne's gray (mix in white where the light is reflected).The knobs locate the darkest tone in the composition and the whitish green of the leeks, the lightest.

▶ **7** Here our artist is doing two things at the same time. First, he's fine-tuning the colours on the chopping board with a browny grey – a lighter version of the ochre mix from step 5. The No.6 long flat brush is just the right size and shape for getting between the onions and doing the second job – adjusting the shape of the bowl.

8 Move on, adjusting negative shapes and positives as you go. Notice how the negatives give the positives too – basic art school stuff, but essential.

Here our artist decided the bowl needed filling out. So he used the No.6 filbert brush and Payne's gray to put in a new outline.

9 When the initial excitement with your subject has worn off and the first flurry of activity is over, you can settle down to a cooler, more dispassionate approach – spotting faults and putting them right!

At this stage our artist has corrected the position of the bowl of potatoes but notes that the asparagus need urgent attention.

10 Look at the set-up. The asparagus stick out from the bowl by an amount that is roughly equal to the height of the bowl itself. Now if you look at step 9 you'll notice that the bunch doesn't protrude far enough. So here our artist uses the same brush and colour mixes to redraw the stems and re-indicate the asparagus tips. The important lesson is: where action is called for, don't delay – do something!

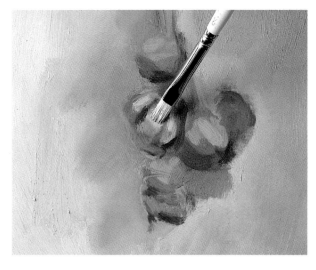

21 Every painting is like a new and exciting journey but there are no short cuts. Don't give up, though – keep concentrating, looking carefully at your subject and revisiting some of the places you've already been to.

Garlic has a silvery skin which is quite reflective, so add highlights where the bulbs catch the light. (Notice how our artist has worked pink into the shadow that was originally a greeny grey, capturing the effect of reflected colour.)

22 Almost a painting in its own right, this little detail was a favourite with our artist.

For the string, try a mix of yellow ochre and white. Touch in the string lightly with the tip of your No.2 flat, then put some shadow on the inside of the loop where the string hangs down from the handle. (Use the same mix you used for the shadow on the handle in step 20.)

23 Put a dense shadow under the chopping board to give this area a really three-dimensional feel. Don't use pure black (shadows rarely are). Instead, make a deep brown mix of black, cadmium red and yellow ochre, and paint the shadow with the No.2 flat brush. Keep a steady hand and try to make the line straight. Really dark shadows like these are the bass notes in the whole composition – the very opposite to the highlights, in fact.

Tip

Grasp a bunch
It's good policy to use touches of the same colour in more than one place. So instead of washing a brush every time you use it, transfer it to your free – non-painting – hand. You can hold several brushes by grasping them like a bunch of flowers. When you need the same colour, simply pick out the right brush.

SOLVE IT

Decant your turps

Throwing away dirty turps can be an expensive business if you clean your palette and brushes regularly. The answer is to save dirty turps in a jar and then let it stand overnight. The following day, you should find that the paint has settled to the bottom. It's then an easy matter to decant the clear turps gently into a clean jar.

◀ 24 You might be tempted to bring your painting to a hurried conclusion by hastily painting the curtain – don't! The curtain veils the window – the light source – and the way in which light shines through, and from behind the curtain, governs how the whole group is lit.

Look at the set-up and you'll see that although the stripes are red, they vary in tone depending on how the light falls on them. In some places they're darker than others – so too are the creamy stripes between. Notice how the stripes vary in width and angle as the material folds. Capture these changes in your painting using your No.2 flat brush and lighter and darker variations of the mixes in step 14.

▼ 25 Although quite pleased with the result, our artist had one criticism – that the subject was a little too complex for the purposes of this exercise. He felt that some of the details – the bowl of potatoes, bunch of garlic or the area around the leeks and handle of the chopping board – would have provided ample material for a painting in their own right.

However, in the finished painting, the warm ground of the MDF board does a fine job of unifying all the components and provides a lively contrast to the cool colours.

At a sitting: Lake Windermere

Beginners are often inhibited by preconceptions of what a good picture should look like. Working on site and in one sitting is an excellent way of responding directly to your subject.

In the academies of the 19th century, painting a landscape in oil was a time-consuming business. Preliminary sketches were done quickly on site, but the real work was completed in the studio in a much more methodical fashion. Rather than working all over the canvas, one section of the painting was worked up each day.

Impressionism in the late 19th century began to change all this. The availability of oil colours in collapsible tubes allowed painting to be done *en plein air*, and this meant artists could respond to changes in the light and make constant revisions all over the canvas. In short, a considered and formal representation of the landscape was replaced by an immediate and emotional appreciation. (This method of painting is often called *alla prima*, meaning 'at first go'.)

It is in this tradition that our artist decided to paint Lake Windermere. He completed nearly all of the painting on location, only putting in the finishing touches in the studio.

▲**1** Draw the basic composition in thin solutions of viridian, cadmium green and yellow ochre, mixed with lots of turps to quicken the drying. Don't worry about the details, but take care over the general proportions of the hills in the distance, the lake in the middle-ground and the trees in the foreground.

◄**2** Now start to block in the underpainting with the No.6 brush. Start in the foreground using cadmium green, cooled with a touch of cerulean. Then define the crest of the hills with a mix of royal blue, ultramarine and touches of cadmium red. Allow the original yellow to show through in places.

Scrub in royal blue for the sky and use a thin wash of yellow ochre and titanium white for the clouds. Put in the lake with a single stroke of the No.5 brush, using a mix of royal blue, cerulean and titanium white.

◄3 Combine ultramarine and touches of cadmium red to make some dark purples for the heather-covered hills. Work over this colour with a variety of green mixes. Apply the paint in different directions to suggest the uneven undulations of the landscape.

Establish some of the shadows of the trees in front of the lake using a mix of ultramarine and viridian. Also use this mix in small dabs to help define the far edge of the lake. Put in the foreground path with a single stroke of yellow ochre – this provides a pleasing echo of the stroke used for the lake.

YOU WILL NEED

- ☐ *A 24 x 18in stretched canvas*
- ☐ *A palette; an easel*
- ☐ *Poppy oil – this speeds the drying, holds the brushstroke well and is especially suited to light colours*
- ☐ *Turpentine*
- ☐ *Three brushes: No.3 round and Nos.5 and 6 filbert*
- ☐ *Some clean rags*
- ☐ *Ten oil colours: titanium white, yellow ochre, raw sienna, cadmium yellow, cadmium red, cerulean, ultramarine, royal blue, viridian and cadmium green*

►4 Tackle the trees with loose brushstrokes, aiming to describe their general shape rather than individual leaves and branches. Use viridian with a little cadmium yellow for the lighter leaves and with a little ultramarine for the darker leaves. Work with slightly thicker paint here, using less turpentine.

►5 Continue working up the light and dark foliage, always bearing in mind the light source. Then block in the landscape quite quickly to give the picture a free and lively quality. Check your painting every now and then by viewing the canvas from a distance. Note that the use of warmer colours in the foreground helps enhance the sense of depth.

▶**6** Concentrate now on the distant hills and the sky. Block in the hills on the right with mixes of royal blue and ultramarine – these act as cool base colours, accentuating the aerial perspective. Also use very thin solutions of these mixes over the clouds to tone down some of the rather warm yellows and browns.

◀**7** Work up the sky by applying royal blue with your finger. Work back into the clouds to soften their outlines and create a sense of movement.
　Add some cadmium red to the blue and apply this to the base of the clouds to give them a menacing, rain-bearing appearance.

▶**8** Continue putting darker tones on the sky, trying to pick up some of the colours of the landscape. For instance, try adding yellow ochre with the No.3 hog brush – this picks up the yellow path in the foreground. To prevent this echo from appearing too crude and contrived, work the yellow ochre into the surrounding cloud colours.

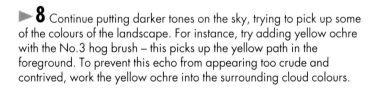

◀**9** The picture is now taking shape. Note how the sense of perspective is enhanced by the different brushstrokes. The large, bold brushstrokes of the foreground leap forward while working and blending the paint wet-in-wet in the background makes the hills recede.

10 Now you need to focus on details. Try, for instance, to distinguish between the shapes and colours of different trees. Add some paler tones on the trees from a palette of viridian, cadmium green, cadmium yellow, yellow ochre and titanium white. Use very little turpentine and poppy oil and keep readjusting your mixes to achieve a subtle range of colours.

Tip

In the clouds
When working *alla prima*, you can easily get carried away with bold and

vigorous brushwork. But this can be unsuited to conveying the airiness of clouds. It's a good idea to use a clean rag to soften the brushwork and blend the colours of the clouds.

11 Prevent the trees from appearing pasted-on by allowing some background to show through the leaves. If you find that the trees are becoming too dense, apply some background colour over them. Then delicately redefine the trees over the new, strong background colour. Here, our artist is using a mix of cadmium yellow with cadmium green to put in a grassy background colour.

12 Vary your palette to distinguish between different species of trees. The soft, delicate leaves of the silver birch on the right are suggested by mixes of royal blue, cadmium green and titanium white. Note also how shadows – created from raw sienna with touches of ultramarine and viridian – have been set against the lighter tones to give the tree a three-dimensional appearance.

►13 Continue using this last dark mix with the No.5 filbert to build up the shadows in the far distance and also to define the edge of the lake. Even though it occupies a small area of the picture, the lake has now become very prominent. The white water shows up very well when surrounded by dark colours.

◄14 The introduction of new colours into the landscape now calls for a re-assessment of the sky. Work in a mix of titanium white and a touch of cadmium yellow with the No.6 brush to bring the cloud nearer to the horizon.

Feel free to merge the paint with the top of the mountains to give an indistinct edge. This helps give the idea of the damp atmosphere.

►15 You can now turn to the finishing touches – but bear in mind you don't want too much detail. Here the artist's aim is not so much to depict the view as exactly as possible but rather to capture the sensation of standing alone, overlooking a rain-soaked landscape.

Use the No.3 brush to put in a very thin stroke of cadmium green and viridian on the lake. Then overlay neat titanium white. The thick broken paint glancing across the canvas conveys the foaming, wind-churned waves.

►**16** Rework the foliage of the fir trees to separate them from the broad-leaved trees. The fir trees' foliage requires a cool mix of ultramarine and viridian; apply it with fluid downward strokes of the brush.

▼**17** At this stage, the on-site painting is finished. But when you view your painting with fresh eyes at home, you may well find it needs a little more attention in one or two areas. It is a good idea to use retouching varnish on the parts needing more work so that the colours are restored to their original value.

Be careful not to overwork the painting, though, and lose the vitality of working *alla prima*. The painting relies on the looseness created by bold brushstrokes and the wet-in-wet application of paint. This technique implies that the light and weather conditions are constantly changing – while some landscapes give the impression of timelessness, as if they will always appear just as they have been depicted, our artist's picture suggests that nature is in continuous flux.

Index

Acknowledgements

Artists

9 Rosemary Davies, 10-14 Stan Smith, 16-18 Bridgeman Art Library; 19(t) Bridgeman Art Library, 20 John McCombs, 29 John McCombs, 30-32 Ian Sidaway, 45 Moira Huntly, 46-50 Stan Smith, 51 Bridgeman Art Library/Musée d'Orsay, 52-56 Ted Gould, 57-64 Madge Bright, 67-70 John Denahy, 71-76 Caroline Penny, 78-82 Stan Smith, 83 Arthur Neal, 84-90 Madge Bright, 91-94 Kate Gallwey, 95-98 Bo Hilton, 99-104 Anne Wright, 105(t) Brenda Holtam, (b) Dennis Gilbert, 106-110 Dennis Gilbert, 111-120 Tig Sutton, 121-126 Victor Willis.

Photographers

Our thanks to the following photographers: Julian Busselle, Ian Howes and Nigel Robertson.